IN A SPECIAL LIGHT

To Irene and Willy

Eliz Bode
Nov. 13, 2006

IN A SPECIAL LIGHT

Elroy Bode

TRINITY UNIVERSITY PRESS
SAN ANTONIO

Published by Trinity University Press
San Antonio, Texas 78212

Jacket design by Erin Kirk New
Book design by BookMatters, Berkeley

♾ The paper used in this publication meets the minimum
requirements of the American National Standard for
Information Sciences—Permanence of Paper for Printed
Library Materials, ANSI Z39.48-1992.

Some pieces in this book were originally published in
the *Texas Observer, Nova, Southern Living,* and the El Paso
Herald-Post. These works are reprinted with permission.

Library of Congress Cataloging-in-Publication Data

Bode, Elroy, 1931–
  In a special light / Elroy Bode.
    p. cm.
    ISBN-13: 978-1-59534-026-9 (hardcover : alk. paper)
    ISBN-10: 1-59534-026-2 (hardcover : alk. paper)
    1. El Paso (Tex.)—Description and travel. 2. Landscape—
Texas—El Paso. 3. El Paso (Tex.)—Social life and customs.
4. El Paso (Tex.)—Biography. 5. Texas Hill Country
(Tex.)—Description and travel. 6. Landscape—Texas—
Texas Hill Country. 7. Texas Hill Country (Tex.)—Social
life and customs. 8. Texas Hill Country (Tex.)—Biography.
9. Bode, Elroy, 1931– 10. Authors, American—Biography.
I. Title.
F394.E4B63 2006
976.4'96—dc22   2006022789

10   09   08   07   06   /   5   4   3   2   1

For my daughter, Deborah, and in memory of my son, Byron,
and also for
Mary Ann Maier
Marian Haddad
Steve Kunert
Ed Patrykus

Contents

PART ONE

El Paso

Earth-Life

I need the earth-life, the ordinary countryside moment, but I cannot make this deep affection seem important to others. On occasion friends look indulgently with me toward the trees or fields that I am showing them, my arm thrown out expansively as we take in the view. They nod, they make affirming comments—try to seem tolerant of my preoccupation with "nature," as they tend to call it—but clearly what is there before us does not mean very much to them, will never count as anything fundamental to their lives.

I need the El Paso countryside. I need to hear the call of redwing blackbirds from salt cedars along an Upper Valley canal. I need to stand in a pecan grove and feel the breeze that moves through it—a breeze that reminds me of other breezes in other trees in other, almost forgotten, times. I need to see stretches of plowed land where, in the distance, humans are reduced in scale and become of no greater importance to the eye than a rooster in a yard, a tractor in a field.

I walk about on farmland roads and I have an urge to say, We are together, these, my silent friends under the sun: the yellow jackets investigating the fenceline grasses, lightly touching—almost kissing, it would seem—the stems and seeds; the leisured, midafternoon drifting about of white fluff from the cottonwood trees; the green June corn and the yellow squash in an old man's backyard garden; the flock of pigeons wheeling upward, coasting, settling again in their smooth formation to sit together in their pigeon community on a telephone wire; the rows of early summer cotton spread across a field like green spokes of a gigantic wheel.

I look, too, at distant trees bordering the fields, and they seem to be offering quiet respirations to the countryside. Their tree-shapes lift, flow, move about, shimmer in the ocean swells of warm summer air, then settle back within the contours of their passive greenery.

The earth: it is as though I were born to be next to it, to see what is growing there—to feel friendly toward the grass on the ground, limbs on a tree.

I walk, I smile, I am rewarded. This valley land—these fields within their mountain borders—is my sun-blazed heaven. I need no other.

Rabbiting

We had two dogs in our shady backyard, but we had a rabbit there too, in her pen, in a corner of the yard. We got her, a just-born little thing, and cared for her, gave her more than adequate space in a pen that we built. The rabbit—female, we thought—dug a hole for herself underneath the rock wall between us and the neighbors and she went down into it—properly rabbitlike—at night or when it rained. We fed her rabbit food and slices of apple and carrot, and had a rabbit-crap pan she agreed to use, and we emptied it daily. In short, we gave the rabbit a good life and a safe one.

Every day the two dogs went up to the screen wire of the pen and sniffed the rabbit and renewed their acquaintance with her. They seemed satisfied with their properly divided territories: rabbit secure on the inside of her pen, dogs still in possession of their large enough backyard.

One day—I can't remember how it came about—we decided that the rabbit might enjoy some extra freedom and the dogs might actually leave her alone—might not corner her and turn her into a lifeless bundle of fur. So we let the rabbit out, and the rest is history.

We stood nearby, of course, and severely cautioned the dogs, who at first quivered and couldn't quite believe their eyes as the rabbit moved blithely among the rosebushes and lantana and bougainvillea. We stood and watched; we were poised to intervene.

Each afternoon we tested the backyard dynamics before

going into the house and watching through the screen door, ready to dash outside at the first sign of the dogs saying Enough of Niceness and bolting over to chew the rabbit raw. We kept stretching the time that the rabbit was out of her pen. We turned our backs on the yard—sort of—and then looked quickly to see what was happening. Nothing was. The dogs were dozing on the cement porch, and the rabbit was either chewing at the trunk of the almond tree or lying full-length among the geraniums.

And so it went.

As a family ritual, so to speak, we began letting the rabbit out of her pen just before dark. The dogs paid her no mind and went on sleeping. The rabbit first cavorted a bit, glad to get the kinks out of her legs, and then went about her business in the yard—eating a rose leaf here, an elm twig there. The only time we had to open the back door was when the rabbit started annoying the dogs. She sniffed them—irritating them enough to make them rise to their feet—then stayed at their heels and chased them around the yard in circles. They really didn't like that, so I finally had to yell, "Leave the dogs alone!" The rabbit usually minded me, although there seemed to be an in-your-face twist to her hop as she turned away. She would scratch hard at grass roots beneath the almond tree and then, rather luxuriously, stretch out on her belly in a damp cool spot.

The dogs were always glad—and so were we—when she finally settled down.

Dee

I thought of him as D'Artagnan—Dee for short. He was my friend for twenty-five years. Dee drank, and finally, after decades of punishing his body, he died an alcoholic's death. Everyone who knew him, and cared about him, was concerned about his problem; and everyone kept saying, "One of these days . . ." When Dee was fifty-seven, the day finally came.

But his drinking, though central to his life and fate, was not why friends would remember him. Dee had élan vital: it flowed through him like a raw, invisible current. Some of us, like Prufrocks, might measure out our lives in coffee spoons. Not Dee. He roared, stalked, danced, yea gamboled through the years. He was a force—whether whomping up a huge salad in his Ruidoso cabin or bellowing out old songs with friends around a neighbor's piano. He savored the pleasures of living; he had an appetite for good food, good talk, good sex, good buddies. He liked presenting himself and his enthusiasms to the world. Dee was an advocate rather than an observer: a partisan, an actor, a clown. He never held back out of faintheartedness or a sense of middle-class decorum. He made waves. And he was the focus of every party (until, of course, he passed out on the living room floor—at which point fellow revelers simply stepped across his outflung arms and prostrate body and kept the party going).

Even as I write these words, I half-expect Dee to interrupt me. He was never one to suffer the sidelines very long.

He thrived on being the center of attention and, if possible, would have tried to upstage his own funeral—moving among the mourners in his Groucho Marx half-crouch, jabbing a forefinger in the air, telling a joke about why it takes three Aggies to fill one casket and perhaps doing a mock buck-and-wing beside his own grave site. Sanctimonious, he was not.

I remember, too, those early Sunday mornings when I would hear him in my front yard, announcing himself with his loud, incredibly acrobatic whistling. He would not stop on the front porch and ring the doorbell as others would. He would bounce—or stride, however his walk should be described—into the front room and right on back to the kitchen, calling out "BO-DE" as if everyone in the world was, or should be, up at eight o'clock on Sunday morning, ready to go. I never quite knew what he wanted during those long, rambling talks, but as he perched on the high kitchen stool—coffee cup trembling in his hand—it was obvious that Dee was a man in need. He was unsure, uncharacteristically vulnerable. He was looking for something, and I think we both knew he would never find it. It was just too deep in him, in his past.

It was a hard lesson, but I learned it: There are those who come into our lives who are both flawed and gifted, and we can't have the gifts without the flaws. They are often not easy to get along with; they can cause as much pain as they bring pleasure. But they are once-in-a-lifetime people — intensely memorable.

Dee was such a person. He was our Upper Valley Musketeer — carrying no sword, wearing no fancy clothing (except, occasionally, a jaunty cloth cap or stylish panama hat), but charged with vitality, blessed with versatility: a Man for All Seasons.

Upper Valley Night

I stopped my car and began walking beneath roadside trees. The sun was down; night was coming. From inside the houses lamps shone dimly through the curtains out into the yards. The long day of summer heat was past now, and a coolness was in the air, along with the smell of honeysuckle, faint and moist.

I liked to come here near the fields and canals, near the Rio Grande, liked to look across into one of the narrow lots and see the silhouettes of horses, the graceful arc of their necks as they bent down to the grass. I liked the sense of an almost rural community—the blending of houses and yards and porch lights and greenery and twilight. I felt I could always renew myself here. I could breathe in the air and get back to a kind of innocence.

Night came, yet it was not just specifically night in the Upper Valley. It was the night of any place after dark at the edge of any town. The pale nighttime sky had its first scattering of stars. Doors shut in the distance; dogs barked; children's voices drifted in from nearby streets. Somewhere a peacock screamed, and then screamed again. And as I listened I became aware of the steady, hypnotic sound of tree frogs. Soon crickets added their own rhythmic chorus from the surrounding fields, and it was as if the night, the land, the world had begun to pulse serenely around me.

A car went along a road beyond an alfalfa field. I

watched the slow movement of the taillights, and they could have been the taillights of a car I had seen fifty years before on a night miles away—a night of childhood, a night in college. In the darkness time seemed to fade, become unimportant, simply disappear. This night, this specific Upper Valley night, was the all-enveloping, changeless every-night of the earth.

I slowed my walk as I came to a familiar neighborhood, and it was here that I began to notice the altered nature of the trees.

I stood beneath them, and it was as if they had somehow taken on more weight—as if they had undergone a metamorphosis, had lost their bright, leafy daytime simplicity and had joined with brooding nighttime forces, belonged now to another world. It was as if imperceptibly, after the sun went down, the placid elms and cottonwoods and sycamores shed their familiar daytime identities as stolid harmless givers of shade and were now their looming after-dark selves: not hostile, not threatening, just more mysterious, more secretive and profound.

They seemed now to be like links between the known and the unknown, the safe and the dangerous; between a poodle in the living room and the wolf in the wild. Their somber masses along the canals and in the quiet yards were the connective element that joined sunny streets and homes and neighborhoods to all that was hidden and unknowable: to life in the jungle and the deep woods, to the forest primeval, to the uncharted lands of the earth before humans had come with their civilizing ways, to the still untamed and undomesticated forces of the dark.

What Hemingway Meant

It was curious. I was there at the kitchen window by the sink, eating peanuts and looking outside. It was about seven-thirty on a summer evening. The house was quiet. I had picked up a book to take to the kitchen while I fixed a rum-and-Coke and began to look out the window into the backyard. There were birds still pecking about in that long subdued hour before dark.

The book was the collected stories of Hemingway, and I was reading one I had read before, "Soldier's Home." I had read almost all the stories in the book at least two or three times; they were from his best writing years when he had wanted "to get the words right." That's what he had said to an interviewer—with some asperity, you could bet—when he was asked why he had rewritten the last page of *A Farewell to Arms* thirty-two times.

I stood at the window, reading the story and eating peanuts and looking at a sparrow moving in the backyard—at the smooth black-and-brown designs on its throat that were like markings a Navajo would make in a rug or a sand painting.

I looked out the window and tried to think how I could write about what I was seeing—the remarkable clarity of that ordinary moment and place: the green yard, the elm trees, the water hose curled in the grass, the sparrow and its intricately marked throat as it poked around on its private errand, the neighbor's tall palm tree jutting into the sky. The sense of the moment, the clear, clean, suspended feel of it, without beginning or end; just there, as if forever—that's what I would want to put down.

I had glanced out the window several times that afternoon—at the same yard, the same trees—but those one and two and five o'clock hours had somehow blurred into this one; their time of day had smoothly, invisibly passed, and now the phenomenon of seven-thirty was in front of me in the growing shadows. Time and the universe—for a brief moment—were visiting in my backyard along with the sparrow, and I was in the kitchen, watching.

I assume I know what Hemingway meant: how hard it is—harder than people think—to get life down on paper and get it right, even a simple thing like a moment of late afternoon, because it is never simple once you start to look at it, once you start to see it as the mystery it really is.

Along Mamie Road

Forty years ago Mamie Road was an Upper Valley cotton field. Now it is an unprepossessing street that dead-ends against the levee of the Rio Grande: a street of occasional windmills in side yards, of morning glory vines winding up wire front fences, of vacant lots filled with knee-deep summer weeds next to well-kept-up houses where Dalmatians lie sprawled beneath globe willows.

There is nothing special about it. I just like its backed-off, mishmash atmosphere: the little garden plots of grapevines and fruit trees and birdhouses — for martins — up on poles; the trailer homes with tentative miguelito vines winding around the doorways; the occasional field of alfalfa; the red pomegranate bushes in a side yard.

Last Sunday I drove out, parked, and checked on things. An elementary school girl was sitting under a tree by her front steps playing a saxophone as I walked by. Her dog sat on its haunches in front of her, listening to the faltering notes of her scale. Nearby, on the screened-in porch, a parrot squawked counterpoints of its own. The dog, head cocked slightly, stayed loyally focused on the sounds of the Little Mistress's sax.

Down the way I looked at horses in a runaround. They chewed hay and twitched their tails against the flies. As I stood at the fence taking in the satisfying smell of their manure dried by the sun — a pleasing aroma on an Upper Valley morning — a barefooted girl on a bike rode up and stopped beside me. "Need any help?" she asked — ten years old, clear eyed, and as sociable and direct as you could want. "No, thanks," I said. "I'm just sort of doing my Sunday visiting." She considered the reply, shifting her weight to her other foot; then, as she began pedaling away, she called back over her shoulder, "Well, if you *need* anything . . ."

It's that kind of street out there in the reaches off west El Paso: a place where strangers are noticed, taken account of, extended a neighborly hand, so to speak, but not viewed with suspicion, not feared.

I walked on past roosters crowing in a back lot, a day's wash hanging on a backyard clothesline, tomato plants set out beside a front walk. It was definitely a live-and-let-live street, Mamie Road.

I went back to my car thinking about perfection: Perfection requires symmetry, the absence of error, blemish, excess. It has an inviolable predictability, a uniformness, a sameness—and frequently, perhaps always, a lack of joy.

Driving home I was glad that I had acquired, somewhere, a liking for the Mamie Roads of the world: a taste for the pleasures of the imperfect.

Plaza People

I sat beneath the downtown plaza trees in the heat, my library book under my arm. I was prepared to sit and read a while, to look up now and then at the regulars who made San Jacinto Plaza their daily resting places—their afternoon open-air homes, their social club beneath the mulberry trees.

I was there among them, the El Paso loners and drifters, old men mainly, Mexican Americans mainly. On a nearby bench a white-haired, white-bearded man slept with his chin on his chest. Another man, beside him, with the brick-red face of a serious drinker, held a section of a newspaper far out in front of him in an effort to read it.

The afternoon preacher was in the public preaching place, walking about in his constrained semicircle. Bible in hand, he shouted his message in Spanish first to one side, then to the other: "Señor!"-this and "Cristo!"-that. The people on the benches did not react. They had other business at hand, the business of sitting in the space of their lives beneath the plaza trees on a springtime afternoon. The preacher was something apart—loud, inescapable— but like an exhibit in a zoo. They had heard him, and the others like him, too many afternoons before. The man could yell and jump about and exhort all he wanted to. They passively regarded the air in front of them and tuned him out.

Two benches away from me a little figure with Down's syndrome sat holding her hands in her lap. She wore a frilly pink-and-white dress and white socks; a small pink-and-white bonnet was tied beneath her chin. Her legs and her small black patent-leather shoes did not quite reach to the concrete.

Her face beneath the bonnet was fair but aged. There were circles underneath her eyes and lines that drew her mouth down. Doll-like, she looked straight ahead. From time to time she rubbed one hand slowly against the other—little pudgy hands. She moved her mouth, as if silently talking to herself, and when she smiled she showed a tooth here and there in an otherwise toothless mouth.

The woman next to her—short, gray-haired: her mother or relative, I assumed—stayed turned away from her as if they were strangers. They sat that way—together but apart, the little doll figure in her frilly dress moving her hands, occasionally sticking her tongue out and then smiling widely. The woman turned away, looked across the plaza to the bus stop, checking the marquee signs on the buses as they came down the street.

Transients crossed the plaza in a slow drifting-about. A man with a frazzled goatee shuffled past, holding a plastic Coke bottle half-filled with water. He was sunk into a dirty gray jacket and a hooded cap that almost covered his eyes. He limped along, leaving his monumental body smell in his wake. He was making his rounds, smiling to himself, chanting in a breathy whisper, "The Ayatollah, *yes* . . . the Ayatollah, *yes* . . ."

Behind me, on the western corner of the plaza, a man in a neat turned-down golfer's hat, light-blue knit shirt, and pressed denim pants sat on the edge of a tree planter. He leaned slightly forward on his aluminum cane, facing the sun, singing songs from Broadway shows: "You and the night and the music . . ."

Poised on the planter's edge, not concerned with the people hurrying past him on their way to the bus stop, the man moved easily, smoothly—one could say professionally—from one song to the next, crooning in a tremulous baritone to the sidewalk pigeons eating the spilled remains of popcorn: "If I loved you, time and again I would try to say . . ."

I closed my book, got up to leave. I was walking south across the plaza when I saw him: another of the downtown regulars. He was near the Coke-and-hotdog stand, sitting on the wall beneath the small oak tree. He wore his floppy, unlaced shoes, his dirty coat, dirty pants. His thinning brown hair was wild; his beard was scraggly. He sat blinking into the heat.

He was hunched over, his mouth open, an unlit cigarette clenched in his big, broken false teeth. He held a ruined packet of paper matches in his hand, but he did not attempt to light the cigarette. He just sat, squinting into some desolate dead place in front of him. Brief explosive sounds came from his mouth, as if a small air brake kept releasing inside him: "Chee . . . chee . . . chee . . . chee."

From time to time he moved his arm in a deliberate, sweeping gesture, his hand and wrist starting to crawl in the air before him: the hand opening, stretching, as if seeking the outline of some forgotten shape. The fingers clutched and contorted, like a spider in its death throes, as the hand turned at the wrist, over and around and over again. He would drag the hand back to his coat and sit there, his mouth bared in a grimace like a chimpanzee's, the cigarette clamped in his oversized teeth.

After a while he got up and began to walk in a measured, tight circle, around and around beside the hotdog stand. His circling was slow, dreamlike, as if he were in a trance. The people waiting nearby seemed accustomed to him. They did not stare as he drifted toward the street, stopped at the curb as if it were the precipitous edge of the earth, and then turned back to the safety of his constant circling. Even when his pants had sagged down his thin hips—to his groin, to the point that he was half-exposed—the people sat on their benches in the heat and looked past him, respecting the privacy of one in their midst who was damaged, harmless, beyond comment, beyond hope.

The Barbershop

It's always a bit of a shock to realize that every child represents the history, the potential—and the fate—of the human race.

Last Saturday morning in Manny's Barbershop I saw a dark-haired boy of ten or so sitting in the barber chair, his body wrapped in white cloth and his head left bare like a piece of sculpture on display. He was an ordinary-looking kid, and as I looked at him, profiled against the back mirror, I thought about some of the men of distinction I had read about and admired. They had probably sat, as children, in a home-town barber chair just as this boy was doing, and they were just as long-suffering as he was— wrinkling his face from time to time against the stray bits of hair tickling his nose. I could visualize a ten-year-old Garrison Keillor in the 1940s sitting stoically as the barber in a small Minnesota town clipped and combed him. He would have seemed no more remarkable than the dark-haired boy in Manny's chair.

There he is, I thought: one more neighborhood kid, one more developing human consciousness born into the stupendousness of the universe. He sits there like a miniature Roman dignitary in his white sheet, paused for a moment in his human adventure, periodically making faces of displeasure at himself in the mirror.

When he stepped down from the chair, he gloomily inspected his reflection, paid Manny, walked out the door: future physician, lawyer, con man, race car driver—who could say? Freshly trimmed around the ears, he was headed down the sidewalk in flopping Adidas to his fate: to grow up, grow old, die; to return, like fine bits of sweepings from the barbershop floor, his little cluster of molecules to the eternal flow of the cosmos.

Skateboarders

When I came out of the 7-Eleven, a half dozen of them were leaning against it; others were taking turns jumping the curb of a sidewalk nearby. With their turned-around caps, punk haircuts, droopy short pants, and old-fashioned black tennis shoes, they were like urbanized Huck Finns. I was surprised at how much I liked them.

The public has never been too comfortable with skateboarders. Maybe it is just their demeanor—not exactly cocky but not Boy Scout winsome either: standoffish, vaguely indifferent to conventional behavior. And they always seem to be halfway down a culvert, halfway up in the air, sometimes disdainfully coasting in the street with cars headed toward them.

The kids at the 7-Eleven were not big guys, not the beefy jocks who fill guard and tackle slots on a football team. They were slight: nifty and shifty. They were foot-folks who had dedicated themselves rather admirably to the pursuit of their curious art. They kept doing their midair twists and seemed to enjoy being at off-angles, being briefly airborne—liking their mastery over curbs and inclines and stairs. They were private members of a satisfying cult working toward private ends. Having no rafts, no Mississippi to float down on a summer afternoon, they seemed content to make do with the unglamorous concrete that El Paso city streets had to offer.

Love in Smokey's Barbecue

I was sitting near them at a rear table. His arm was across her back, and his hand rested at her neck beneath her long black hair. She sat pivoted in her chair, facing him. They had finished with their barbecue, and now they were free to resume being young lovers, content in their talking. She smiled often; sometimes she laughed. He sat composed, unmoving, attentive to her. Half-turned, he murmured assent to what she had to say: she, his pleasant-faced companion; she, with her bright eyes, dark eyebrows, dark eyelashes; she, with her strong and classic profile, a face on a coin.

As she moved her hands from time to time—shaping her ideas there between their faces that almost touched—he would give a light little laugh in agreement with a point she had made. But even then he did not move, did not alter his rapt focus on her.

Romeo and Juliet—doomed—did not make it into old age. But as I looked at these two lovers—he with his Nordic blond hair and eyebrows, she with her Hispanic dark hair and light brown skin—I thought they surely would. I could see them years from now: his yellow tufts of a chin beard faded into white, her dark hair still flowing across her shoulders but streaked with gray. She would be talking, of course; she would still be bringing him her vitality. And he would be there beside her: staunch, unwavering, the fixed planet to her ever-circling moon.

Rhythms

I have a world that brings me beauty and joy: the physical, shining world of sun on the land and berries on a bush.

Yesterday, on my walk, I was like a king of all that I possessed. But I was not merely a "walker," and that is a hard thing to tell: how it is possible to become the thing you see and be filled, expanded, pleasured by what is around you.

As I walked, swallows swooped above the blue-green stretch of alfalfa and ants made their way along the Ant-Autobahn of the bare roadside. In the distance a man in blue overalls and a floppy Farmer Jones straw hat mowed his huge back lot, back and forth, lost in the hypnotic roar of his machine. And in the exact middle of a pasture three cows lay at rest under the bright, cloudless sky. Half-hidden among tall, yellow-tipped weeds, they chewed with the serene assurance of Hindu deities keeping the universe properly on course.

Just past a shimmering row of Lombardy poplars I stopped at a barny, rural place—my kind of place. A dozen or so goats and sheep ambled about, snorting dust from their noses, nibbling at stray strands of grass, just being peaceable, shade-sharing buddies under their tin roof. Bantam hens pecked and scratched in their chicken dirt-dance and drifted through sunlight and shadow like brown-and-white speckled ships. A family of gray ground squirrels began to play chase in and out of a shed. White butterflies floated beneath the chinaberry trees—brief touches of delicate noontime, summertime grace.

I do not know why I am so comfortable among tools and oil drums, rusted and weathered through the seasons; among bales of hay and dried manure; among animals and birds. All I know is that I could have climbed through the fence and sat on a stack of old tires and stared out at nothing in particular the rest of the afternoon.

Such places, I suppose, are where nervous city rhythms have disappeared—where tree rhythms, earth rhythms, mockingbird rhythms shape the day; where the slightly buried memories of a person's life can reassert themselves and be reclaimed. Where a person, freed of onerous duties and burdens, can be in touch once more with essentials: the way a hawk dives, the way a rooster's shrill call rises, curves, fades—and leaves a vacancy, an expectation, a curious longing.

Essence

One afternoon I paused at a clump of elm tree saplings growing along a canal. I looked at one of the green stems and at the leaves arranged on it, each leaf a duplicate of the other, the veins finely etched. I pulled off part of the shoot and stared at each leaf, actually stared into the leaf, trying to find there—exposed, somehow—the essence of life.

I thought about the leaf and how it had grown so perfectly into the shape of itself—the way all living things, at the proper time and in the predictable manner, become themselves—and I could not help asking my absurd question: what was the leaf's "meaning"? I glanced down the canal. On each side of it the cottonwoods and elms were exploding into their green summer life with millions of leaves. My question mocked me: what was the meaning of *those* leaves?

In the distance, at the bend of the canal, two blue-jeaned teenagers held each other, their bodies fused within the deep shade of an elm. Secret afternoon lovers, they clutched and swayed—the irresistible need that drove their kisses no different from the force that had caused the elm leaves to bud and ascend one behind the other up the green stem.

Leaf life, love life: each obeying its own mindless urgencies.

I stared again at my canal leaf, trying to read in the neat, symmetrical shape a clue that would let me penetrate, somehow, nature's invisible hieroglyphics. But it offered me no answers, of course. I could stare at it until I went blind and I would never see into the heart of it: into the hidden pulse of creation.

In Clint

I took my weekly late-afternoon drive down to Clint. I could see the Clint water tower as I turned off the interstate from El Paso and went down into the Lower Valley. The cotton and alfalfa fields, the distant mountains in Mexico, the desert space—they began to work their late-afternoon chemistry on me. I passed farmhouses, lone cottonwoods, canals. The farm-to-market road had a worn, comforting shine, like the skin of an elephant.

At the park across from the Catholic church, I stopped beneath a row of elms and read for a while. I liked to do that: just sit in my car and read and drink coffee from the thermos on the front seat and now and then look out the window. Boys were throwing a ball around in the park. Roosters crowed in a nearby yard. The faint smell of barbecue was in the air.

I began my walk through the neighborhood. At the side of the churchyard a man filled plastic jugs from the church water fountain and put them into the back of his pickup. Across the street the old man and his wife were sitting, as usual, on their front porch in straight-back wooden chairs, watching the man fill the jugs to take to his home in a nearby *colonia*. The porch seemed to give them their daily life: shade in the morning, sun in the afternoon, the cars that drove slowly past, the sparrows in the tall churchyard trees. They nodded to me as I walked by. We were familiar sights to each other.

I passed the Clint houses and their small yards, and it was as if they belonged to me, as if I had earned the right to incorporate them into my own life because I took such satisfaction in seeing them there week after week: the dogs behind their fences, the Virgin Mary decorations beside the front doors, the small boys chasing each other around chinaberry trees, the trucks in the driveways with their Dallas Cowboys stickers in the rear windows.

On the street that led north out of town, doves were sitting on the telephone wires—orderly, like members of a club, facing west and the lowering sun. I kept walking, past pens of horses and sheep, and when I came to the open space of the cotton fields I stood for a long time, once again feeling that I should make a pronouncement of some kind in the presence of such a wideness of sky, such a stretching out of the land. I wanted to be equal to such spaciousness. But I was not, had never been, and I was forced, once more, to turn around, empty of any kind of summing up.

I walked back into Clint—to the yards and gardens, the shade trees, the silent houses and silent windows, the side streets and long-abandoned stores. I sank into small-town late-afternoon-ness. I stood at a street corner as the sun rays angled in from the horizon and lit up carpet grass in one yard, cast long shadows across the sidewalk in another. I remained there—waiting, receptive, as if I had lost something important in just such a place long ago and, if I remained still and unobtrusive, I might catch a glimpse of it again, might manage to reclaim it and let a puzzling, incomplete part of me finally become whole.

Bird-Life

Each morning I went in the backyard and put grain in the feeder that hung beneath the almond tree. Then I went back into the house to stand at the kitchen window and watch the birds. They had been patiently waiting in the surrounding trees—waiting while I fed the dogs, set a sprinkler on low, watered the tomato plants, filled the bird feeder with scoops of mixed grain from my bucket. They waited as I gazed at the sky, the trees, the morning. Then finally—*finally*—I went inside and they were free to swoop in from their hiding places, to materialize in the air as soon as I closed the door.

Three or four sparrows zoomed in and sat on the narrow ledge around the feeder, pecking away with spirit. They were fairly careless eaters and constantly knocked grains down to the grass. Soon it was double-decker feasting, with the sloppy sparrows working away at the feeder and several Mexican doves cleaning up the scatterings on the ground below.

Before long Big Lennie, the white-tailed dove, made his appearance. Beautiful and graceful in flight, Lennie simply didn't fit on the narrow ledge of the feeder. He couldn't find any footing and was like an elephant trying to balance on a shopping cart. Once he did get a precarious claw hold, he was still out of luck: he couldn't figure out a way to get his beak to the grain on the swinging feeder. So he just sort of danced a while, looking perplexed but also seeming to enjoy the ride well enough—like an overgrown kid on a merry-go-round—until he gave up and joined the crew down below.

Birds continued to gather in the yard. The white-winged doves settled on the grass and grew content by the birdbath. Stationary for long moments, they became almost sybaritic as they slowly stretched up a wing like an elegant gray fan and began to luxuriate in the sun and fine spray from the water sprinkler. The small Mexican doves found their own places near the rosebushes, fluffed their feathers, pecked in the grass and dirt, jostled among each other for their proper bird space, and then, settled, they looked about, alert to possible dangers but finding only sun and breeze and shade on their pleasant riviera.

The bird-club members were forced to yield up their cool shadowed territory when the morning spoilsport sailed in. The black grackle walked about, seizing the territory with his beak opened aggressively like miniature scissors—a bold descendant of his pterodactyl kinsmen of eons past. Swaggering in his spraddle-legged gait—truly, like a bird with hemorrhoids—he poked and gobbled in the grass, then marched over to one of the dog bowls, found a leftover morsel of Kibbles 'n Bits, took it to the birdbath, swished it about—staining the clear water—and flapped away over the fence.

The yard was quiet and empty for a while. Nothing moved. A red-throated house finch darted to the hummingbird feeder outside the kitchen window, rode it awkwardly for a while, abandoned it, and reentered the cozy enclosure of an elm, where he sat in speckled shade like a little sheik comfortably settled within his tent of leaves.

It was then that I heard the Voice of the Airwaves: the prince himself, Mikhail Mockingbird. He was sitting on the top of an Italian cypress in the yard next door—on his perch with a view. He sang and sang. He was the solitary artist of the Upper Valley morning, alone with his creations, and for the next half-hour or so he offered to lesser songsters his magnificent repertoire.

Earl

My friend Earl was a loner, but over the years he told me enough about himself that one night I decided to try to write about him—to create, if possible, a word portrait that might capture the essence of this intense, haunted, often troubled man.

On Saturday afternoons Earl liked to take his dog, Lobo, and a six-pack of beer and drive down a Lower Valley road until he reached a place where he could sit in the shade of a culvert and look across the desert heat into the mountains. He was at home there with Lobo and his beer and his rusted Plymouth. He enjoyed the cavelike privacy of the culvert, with the swallows darting in and out, and the miles of greasewood that stretched beyond the barbed-wire fence. He liked the sense of distance and the companionship of his solitude.

He would drink a can of beer and listen to the quick echoing sounds of the swallows in the culvert and he would grow Saturday-afternoon sad. He would think of the little town in Chihuahua that he used to go to with his wife before she died. He remembered her laugh, her pert ways. "Esperanza . . . Esperanza." He said her name out loud and wiped tears away with his big-knuckled hand, and as he reached for another beer the memory of their arguments—loud, harsh, bitter arguments—became blurred by a drifting wave of sentiment.

Earl would sit, Lobo dozing at his side, and he would think back to the cold winter days when he was growing up on the farm in Wisconsin—his father stalking about the pens in one violent rage or another, cursing the pigs, cursing the weather, cursing Earl, striking out at him with his fists or a hammer or whatever happened to be in his hand. He thought of his mother, as grim and fiercely unhappy as his father, taking her resentments to mass each week and then beating at Earl with her own hammer of Catholicism year after year.

He thought of his days in the army—the long drunken weekends in Germany—and the days with his wino friend Aldo, who wandered with him after their discharge through the bars of Milwaukee.

Lost days, painful days.

"My God, my God!" he would cry out, gritting his teeth, slamming his fist into the sandy ground. Lobo would twist about, look up at him, wag his tail a bit, go back to dozing.

The afternoon wore on, the shadows stretched out, and Earl sat beside the culvert until the sun went down. Of all the places he could be—of all the places he had been—he was glad he was here. He listened to the quail calling in the greasewood and the bullfrogs beginning to tune up in the canal down the way.

The border, this huge stretch of desert, was his place of

peace now. He knew he was lucky to have drifted out of the nagging horrors of the North and down into the Southwest. His memories would always be bad, would never go away, but he could handle them here among the mountains, in the calming distances and the space.

Two O'Clock in the Heat

It was 106 degrees at two o'clock, but I wanted to walk in the heat, in the sun-illumined countryside. I pulled my car off the highway, got my straw hat from the backseat, and started down a side road past scattered houses and fields.

Two o'clock on a June day was as intimate to me as any secret: the clean-swept dirt by the side door of an adobe house, the faint smell of road tar, the distant hum of a tractor, the heat-dazed stare of chickens—beaks open, panting—as they stood together in chinaberry shade, the green rows of corn turned a deeper green in the steady summer sun.

I walked, glad to be squinting and sweating because the earth was hot and bright and I was more alive because of it. I walked, and I felt as cleansed as a Greek of old—as if my body were being buried in sand and then scraped thoroughly with a blade.

After a while I crossed to a canal and stood beneath the canopy of a pecan orchard. Doves called from within the trees—gentling the air with their unhurried sounds—and a hummingbird appeared above the surface of the canal. It hovered over the coffee-colored water, then took itself away—showing in its peremptory flash-and-dash that it came like afternoon lightning: as a gift, a marvel.

It was there, near weathered farmland sheds and with a hawk circling overhead—in a place of timeless desert air and desert greenery—that my nagging need for answers welled up again. It was against common sense, but I had never given up on the idea that one day I could simply stop, be still, and know the world, that I could be walking along and come to an ordinary tree or wall or fence on an ordinary road and there I would pull the universe to me.

It seemed I should be able to do that—to find, finally, the Authentic Place and the Authentic Moment, to be so ready, so receptive, so open that I could stand there and have my life and the life of the world finally come together: to touch, to blend, to become one.

I looked west toward the massive, heat-hazed clouds that rose in godly fashion above the horizon. I looked at the sky overhead, pure and blue and impersonal—but there were no epiphanies there, no messages, and no voice from a Burning Bush along the canal.

Just silence, as always. Just the strong presence of the earth and the steady white glare of the two o'clock sun.

Old Mesilla

I wandered into the plaza of Old Mesilla. The sun was out, taking the chill from the October air. The afternoon was subdued and still.

Nothing intruded on the quiet spell of four o'clock.

On the north side of the plaza the Catholic church loomed above the trees, but its outline against the sky was so sharp that it seemed unreal. New Mexico alchemy was at work—the radiantly clear air letting the sun etch the church into the blue background like a laser.

For a long while the plaza itself was a study in shadows—the shadows of the plaza trees, the shadows from the surrounding shops spreading onto the narrow streets.

It seemed to me that a person could possess the plaza, if he wanted to, and take it with him as a charm, the way religious devotees sometimes keep holy relics or anthropologists might keep a treasure from an excavation. Reduced to a pendant, the plaza could be worn as a life memento.

At dusk the sky to the west remained a wide stretch of lingering pastel, as though the earth, shutting down for the night, was doing its best to please those of us who had continued to sit there into the twilight.

Couples began to wander past, then settled onto the benches beneath the elms. A girl on skates went gliding by and began to make leisured circles in the concrete center space of the plaza. As the light faded, the steeple of the church kept its outline against the faint pastel glow.

Across the way at El Patio a combo, warming up for the night's session, began to practice a slow version of "Autumn in New York." The music, muffled but curiously full-bodied, sounded as if it were coming from the far end of a huge, echoing ballroom.

Night came, and we were companionably fused together: the darkness, the moody sounds of the music, the figures on the benches beneath the trees.

Late Afternoon

The day had been mild, the sky clear.

In the distance cows from the nearby dairy were head down in a cornfield, still eating but waiting, too, for the rider on horseback to come along the fenceline and drive them to the dairy stalls before night.

Fifty or so doves sat together on a telephone wire at the edge of a cotton field, their breasts somewhat aglow from the fading November sun.

The Franklin Mountains were stretched along the entire eastern horizon, tapering to the north and the south, as if reaching toward the ends of the earth and, maybe, eternity.

It was a peaceful, suspended moment in the Upper Valley. A cow lowed from far away, an unseen tractor raised a faint cloud of dust, but nothing disturbed the harmony of the fields.

Suddenly—the way a group of children might react at the beach if they had the sudden urge to go for a swim— the doves took off. They left in a wide, sweeping arc to the south until, in a gradually settling line, they curved downward. In a precise way they dipped, as one, and disappeared into the green waves of the cornstalks below.

I walked along Gardner Road toward a dense growth of elms and poplars that followed the irrigation canal. The trees concealed a farmhouse and barns, and for fifty yards or more made an oasis-like contrast to the surrounding expanse of land.

In the path beside the canal I came across a community of anthills sitting like miniature temples in the fine, silky sand. Each hill was nicely scooped out toward the middle, with one side rising higher than the other. I wondered why that was. Maybe, I thought, maybe the higher side was used as a kind of ceremonial balcony, and from time to time the worker ants brought captive aphids to the top and threw them off as ritual sacrifices to their queen. I bent down closer to one of the mounds, but nothing dramatic was going on. A few black ants crawled along, tending to their ordinary affairs, disappearing into the neat hole in the center of the hill.

A few yards down the path a number of small mollusk shells lay half-buried in the sand. They had probably been unearthed when the canal had last been dredged. They were perfectly shaped, white, brown, blue-tinged—some no larger than my thumbnail, others as small as an eraser top. Their delicate markings fanned across the outer sides in beautifully arching symmetries; the insides of the shells were still smooth and glossy.

They lay there, silent little messengers from the salty seas that had covered the Rio Grande basin for millions of years.

Behind the long mesa in the west the sun was spreading its orange glow, and the alfalfa fields had begun to take on a deeper shade of green.

Each fence post, cotton plant, bird on a limb seemed poised, waiting, in the fading light. Out in the fields crickets were beginning their welcoming chorus to the cooling air and the coming darkness. The land was withdrawing from the day.

I did not believe in magic, but as I stood there on the bank of the canal I thought I could understand how humans might have once embraced magical moments. It would have been at such a time as this, when earth and trees and the coming night seemed to take on a power and beauty and mystery that was beyond words, a time when the air itself might seem strangely luring, enchanting, and reason and reality might suddenly be seduced by things unaccountable, unseen.

PART TWO

Teaching

The Page-after-Page

I kept teaching for almost half a century because all those people, not yet grown, kept coming into my room, wherever I was, and seated themselves at desks and looked at me, and I knew that such a place was exactly where I wanted to be.

It was just that simple.

I enjoyed being the teacher who was there when students came into the classroom. I enjoyed greeting them, I enjoyed providing them with work to do—books to read, essays to write, ideas to think and talk about. I enjoyed providing them a place where they could feel comfortable as they learned. I enjoyed knowing that they trusted my intentions and that I trusted theirs.

I taught English, which meant that students frequently wrote about themselves and I read what they wrote.

I was a sucker for the human drama, and that's what I got when students wrote: drama. They revealed themselves on page after page.

The English teacher—the trafficker in language—is pretty much the school's beast of burden, lugging around stacks of compositions and research papers and creative work of one kind or another. The English teacher: a martyr, almost, to the causes of literacy, clear thinking and expression, even moral uplift. The English teacher: a person who believes that what a student has thought or read can best be revealed at the tip of a pen.

Now if such a teacher can create an air of trust in the

classroom, and if students feel they can write openly and honestly about themselves because they believe the teacher is going to be supportive and nonjudgmental, then look out: the emotions of those deceptively inexpressive masks-atop-mannequins will spiral out onto the page—awesomely, like bats in a cave headed toward a crack of light. The Rogelios and Jennifers—who had sat so woodenly and indifferently—often reveal how it is to be who they are.

That kid slumping in his seat at ten-thirty on a Wednesday morning? He wasn't a passive receptacle to be filled with learning. He was a kid in an apartment or house, with his family members, or the lack of them, and what went on in that apartment or house did not simply evaporate when he walked into the classroom.

Why was Julio Balderama so unresponsive morning after morning? Why didn't he hand in assignments? Well, in one of the compositions he did complete he revealed that he worked weekdays from ten at night to six in the morning, came to school, slept from four in the afternoon until eight or so, and went back on the job at ten. "But Julio," I would say, "there's no way you can pass and still work at night." Yeah, sure, Julio knew that, but his mother needed the money and there were no other jobs in sight.

Childhood rape, and abuse, longings and mournings, family deaths and personal deprivations—they were all there on the page-after-page: tales typically told out of school but sometimes for the first time told *in* school, on paper, in an English class by students finally able to reveal a few scenes from their ongoing life stories.

Commitment

The school buildings and playgrounds of my home town were just a block from my house when I was growing up, and I had some good experiences there. I liked school. In the eighth grade I had a mild ambition to become a county agricultural agent—my roots were pretty much in the ranchland and countryside then. But when I graduated from high school, I had become more interested in books than in goats and sheep, although I still had no idea what I was going to "do" or "be." Teaching? Of course not. No self-respecting guy in my high school class would think of announcing to the world: "I'm going to be a teacher!" Teachers were too close at hand, too full of warts and frailties, too much like parents; they were not glamorous enough. To a high schooler, the idea of becoming a teacher was like spending twelve years preparing to jump off the Grand Diving Board of Life—and then jumping, and landing not in the bracing waters of Glory and Fame but in the family bathtub.

So I more or less backed into teaching, looking over my shoulder to scout out the other possibilities. (I guess I should make this point: young people marked by the Urge to Write, as I was, generally have a hard time settling on a career. Whatever it is that makes them want to write also keeps them from making a definite commitment to traditional forms of work.) In college I majored in English and took education courses the same way a person takes out insurance: just in case. Then I graduated from the University of Texas and was hired for my first job. I planned to stay a year, maybe two or three — just long enough for me to figure out what I really wanted to do with my life.

My starting salary was $3,150 — far down the professional pay scale. But that was 1954 when coffee was still a nickel a cup, and I was unmarried, so I managed okay. Of course teachers' pay in Texas had always been rock bottom — low pay and low public esteem defined the territory. Teachers were crippled and blessed by the cliché, "Teaching is its own reward." Yet as with many clichés, there was a truth in it — at least for me.

During those first years of teaching I think I simply liked the smell, the look, the feel of school buildings: cleaning compounds on the wooden floors of small-town schools, incinerator smoke rising from behind the shop building at four in the afternoon, kids chasing each other through the shadows of oak trees by the gym and other kids hitting a worn green tennis ball back and forth on the court.

I taught here and there in Texas, but when I came west to Austin High School in El Paso, I knew I was home. Call it genuine attachment or simply blind loyalty, but I never wanted to teach anywhere else.

Teachers can usually find any number of reasons for

changing jobs: better salaries, more personal or professional pluses in some idyllic Crestwood Knolls, U.S.A. But for me it was satisfying to get out of my car on Memphis Avenue in central El Paso each day and walk toward the familiar front steps. It was like a commitment to a cause or a family.

Tuna Fish

A teacher is necessarily part of the larger world—the world beyond the classroom—and I felt I had to be concerned with the social and political problems of the day. But my way of viewing—or writing about—those issues tended to bring me into conflict or disagreement with others at my school. In the spring of 1966 it caused me to stop eating in the school cafeteria and start bringing a tuna fish sandwich to eat in my room.

At Austin High teachers ate in shifts in a faculty room next to the cafeteria. My shift coincided with a kind of power lunch for coaches and ex-coaches: the principal, a likable ex-coach; an assistant principal, an ex-coach; a counselor, also an ex-coach; and several other male teachers who made the lunch hour into a locker room get-together of Good Old Boys.

I typically drifted in with a book and my lunch tray, sat off to the side, ate, read, and then drifted out. That's the way it went, day after day. After many such weeks and months I had become just about invisible to the others. It was their room, their get-together time.

The noon that I gave up eating cafeteria food started out routinely enough: the Guys came in, trailing deferentially behind the principal, and seated themselves. They ate, offered comments from time to time about sports, school topics, events in the news. At one point, in between mouthfuls, one of the Guys said, "Did you see where Martin Nigger Coon is going to be doing one of his protest marches in that place outside Chicago—Cicero?"

They felt they were safely in their clubhouse.

I wish I could remember the exact words that erupted from my mouth as I rose and delivered my excoriation. I believe they were pretty effective: a fulsome blast delivered, I would like to think, "with steely control." I gave the Guys what-for. I told them, in essence, that I would no longer be eating with them in their racist beanery—something like that—and then took my tray and left.

What lingers is the memory of their reaction: jaws dropped in midbite, they kept looking around the room for the source of the words that had so unexpectedly intruded on their conversation. They had forgotten that I was there and were perplexed at having their meal interrupted.

Maybe my words didn't register. Or maybe it was the case of the elephant not being bothered by the gnat. At any rate, I had tuna fish and Fritos in my room thereafter.

Vietnam

In the fall of 1965 I still did not know what to think about the war in Vietnam. I had coasted along like many Americans, lulled by my ignorance of the conflict. But when I learned that the first antiwar protest in El Paso was going to be led by a University of Texas at El Paso professor and a GI group from Fort Bliss, I wandered over—mainly out of curiosity—to the downtown plaza and watched the small group, holding signs, walk around and around the central alligator pond. I was impressed by their dedication and by the stoic way they handled the crowd's jeers and heckling. I wrote my impressions of the demonstration for the *Texas Observer*.

Two years passed, and by Christmas 1967 I had decided I needed to do something about my ignorance concerning Vietnam. I checked out all the books I could find on the subject from the El Paso public library and from the university. During the Christmas break, after I had done my crash reading, I was convinced that the country was indeed in a terrible "quagmire," as David Halberstam had termed it.

In January I went across the border to sit at the bar of the Florida Club in Juárez and, over Cuba libres, puzzle my way through an ageless human dilemma: What can any one person do, alone, when faced with one of the world's problems? What should I do now, having read what I had read, having come to the conclusions I had come to?

I decided I could at least try to educate a few of my less-than-concerned fellow El Pasoans by writing an analysis of the Vietnam conflict and presenting it, in the form of a paid advertisement, in the *El Paso Times*. At the Florida bar I wrote in my pocket notebook the first paragraph of what finally became a ten-point Statement of Concern: "We the undersigned believe that, as another year of war in Vietnam comes to a close and another one begins, each American citizen is morally obligated to do whatever he can to focus attention on the truth of the war as he sees it..."

With the help of El Paso businessman John Karr, a West Point graduate and member of the ACLU, I was able to raise $600 for the cost of the ad. We located thirty-two people in town—including novelist John Rechy—who were willing to sign it.

Nothing much came of the ad—just a few predictable letters to me questioning my patriotism.

"Hey, Prof, Why Don't You Set Yourself on Fire?"
(1965)

I had not planned to go to the demonstration. I was just downtown loafing and had stopped in at the Hotel Cortez for a haircut. Ordinarily the main Saturday topic would have been football, but not this morning. "I wish they'd turn the boys from Fort Bliss loose on 'em for about a minute," one barber was saying, gesturing with his scissors. "I bet that'd cure those 'protesters.'" There was a general head bobbing of agreement from the straight-backed men in barber chairs. One fat man, reclining for a shave, pulled his steaming towel aside and wheezed, "Punks . . . just a bunch of punks," and slapped the towel back over his face. Barbers and customers nodded again, quite serious and quite in accord.

Well, demonstrations . . . I didn't know. And I didn't know what to think about the El Paso Committee to End War in Vietnam—the ones that were going to demonstrate in the plaza—except that they had the right to exist and have their say and maybe cause people to think a little more deeply about a hell of a complex problem. They were probably about half right and half wrong, just as everyone else who had taken a stand about Vietnam was probably half right and wrong. An undeclared war, and bombings of civilians, and Communist aggression, and self-determination, and loss of Southeast Asia, and

U.S. commitment—nobody seemed to have a single, easy way to make a solution out of all those current phrases. Why not keep thinking about them—hard, and in public.

I paid for my haircut and walked over to San Jacinto Plaza to wait. I had never seen any kind of protest group in action before except for a few bored Mexican American men who had once picketed the Hilton Hotel. The antiwar demonstration was set for one o'clock, but at twelve-fifteen the plaza was just as it always had been: a fine place to be sitting in on a pleasant fall day. Old men in coats were out taking the sun, couples were idling around the center alligator pond, and barefooted Mexican boys with homemade shoeshine boxes were trying to drum up trade. Japanese and Korean student officers from Fort Bliss were snapping pictures; Negro students from Texas Western College were waiting for their bus. An old gypsy woman was asleep on the grass.

I found it hard to believe that this cosmopolitan little park was suddenly to become a hotbed of violent passions. On dozens of Sunday afternoons I had sat listening to plaza evangelists exhort the crowd—and no one had ever jumped up, infuriated by a holy roller's interpretation of the Bible. It would be interesting to know if Vietnam could strike closer to a man's vitals than a concept of God.

For the next twenty minutes or so things went along routinely—pretty much the way any crowd would gather for any downtown spectacle. Motorcycle policemen roared up in crash helmets and shining boots, people began standing on flower bed walls to get a better view, traffic thickened in the streets. But gradually you could sense a change in atmosphere. Mingled among the strollers and bench-riders were obvious plainclothesmen who were trying to stand around and look inconspicuous. They puffed narrow cigars and ambled about, the ridges of their shoulder holsters showing through their coats. Several Veterans of Foreign Wars were beginning to pass out miniature American flags.

A squinting, burr-haired Mexican American man with an "I'm Happy" button on his lapel walked about searching for something in the air, on the ground—somewhere. "That's Chuy de la O," a man said, shaking his head. "He'll be trouble for somebody." Little knots of newsmen and photographers had grown together, the newsmen holding cigarettes and sounding dispassionate and articulate. An old man in old man's shoes and khaki pants and a worn-out hat— eighty-five, if a day—was pushing a candy vendor's cart with THE DENVER KID hand-printed in front. He was selling Almond Joys.

I decided that was going to be the tone of our controversial demonstration: Old Mortality, in the guise of the Denver Kid, would sell his Almond Joys and provide a stabilizing element; the eccentric "I'm Happy" guy would go frantically along squinting after his private demon in the crowd and providing us with a Dark Omen; the newsmen would keep everything objective and in focus. It was all going to be a good casual leg-stretch and eye-balling. Minority dissent taken in stride in tolerant El Paso.

The noon was so very pleasant—grass smelling good, sun warm, men moving about leisurely with slung cameras and jutting pipes—that I grew reflective as I waited. Hmmm: public gathering, with a spark of political tension in the air. I hadn't been in Dallas on November 22 but I had seen the pictures, had read.

I found myself automatically looking up at the open windows of the surrounding buildings. Two days before a crank caller had threatened the life of the Texas Western history professor who was to lead the demonstration: I tried to imagine how the windows of the School Depository Building had looked to those gathered below on the grass.

By one o'clock the crowd in the plaza had gathered and was ready. Sidewalks were jammed, cameras were out, the many small American flags were distributed and pinned. (They provided a handy division between the Good Guys and the Bad. Those not wearing flags stood together and made quiet jokes among themselves; they were the definite minority. One college boy told another, "Tonto, I'm glad I brought my silver bullet.")

No one seemed to know what the demonstrators were going to do or say or what sort of impression they would make. Would they look like beatniks; would one of them—maybe that history professor—get up on a box and address the crowd? What kind of people were demonstrators, anyway? This was a new spectator sport, and the crowd was curious.

Waiting, I wondered where Chuy de la O was and what he was going to do. The Denver Kid had stopped by a water fountain to hitch up his pants. Policemen were clearing out the last of the shoeshine boys, causing one man to yell, "Hey, sergeant, how come you're running *them* off? They're not against us—they believe in free enterprise." People laughed.

Finally, across the way, from the direction of the Western Union Building on the northwest corner, here they came: the war protestors. White pasteboard signs had begun to bob underneath the sidewalk elms and the crowd was surging toward them. At first it was not clear what route the protestors were going to take; the crowd kept flowing back and forth uncertainly. Boys gave up good viewing positions on lampposts and then had to fight to regain them; photographers ran this way and that. But the pattern was soon established: the protest group, led by Dr. Richard Trexler, was going to march around a triangle following the northwest sidewalks. They were going to carry signs, look straight ahead, and say absolutely nothing.

Up to that point—the arrival of the demonstrators—I had not been emotionally involved. Not aloof, but content to be merely an onlooker. I had watched the old men in their American Legion caps and social-security-bought cheap orange shoes harangue each passerby. But everything had been about what I had expected. And the woman who had a son fighting in Vietnam would, of course, want her son supported and would express her opinion loudly—I had understood her point of view.

It was only after the protestors had actually begun to walk through the plaza that sweat from my armpits began to drip.

"Hey, professor, I can get some gasoline. Why don't you go set yourself on fire."

"Chick-chick-chick-chick-chick . . . he-rrrre, chickie."

"Where's your hammer and sickle, traitor."

" 'Professor' . . . you're not even fit to teach cowards."

A Mexican American woman at the edge of the crowd started up a barrage that lasted throughout the demonstration. She was a grim hater.

"Sombies!" she hissed, in her thick accent. "No, don't look at nobody; look dead. Well, you might as well be dead. Sombies . . . shickens . . . dodgers."

A man held up a photograph of Khrushchev with a sign that read, "Welcome Comrats."

A thin-faced boy in a white windbreaker with a Texas Western emblem on the front got in his licks from the safety of the crowd. "You're red . . . yellow red." He jammed his hands deep into his jacket, satisfied with his yell, and then looked around carefully for approval from the crowd.

The police stationed along the route were ready for Chuy de la O and eased him away on the marchers' first trip around. Young men with pads and pencils tried to interview the demonstrators as they walked, but the marchers just held their signs and looked straight ahead. Dr. Trexler carried a sign: "Have we asked the Vietnamese?" A girl with long dark hair held a sign saying, "Would Jesus Carry a Draft Card?" A male voice called out, "Hey, baby, did you burn *your* draft card?" and for a moment the girl lost her composure and half-smiled.

Around and around the triangle went the procession, with a red-jawed motorcycle policeman as their escort. The crowd kept talking the situation over, grumbling, jeering, shaking their heads, jeering some more.

"Look at 'em; they couldn't even *lift* a gun."

"Why don't you carry the Commie flag?"

A demonstrator passed carrying a sign reading, "I Want to Know the Truth About Viet Nam." A middle-aged man yelled, "Why don't you go there and find out, chicken?" The crowd began to squawk.

The Mexican American woman in front had not let up on her hissing litany: "skunks . . . traitors . . . sombies."

With sweat pouring down my sides and my head beginning to pound, I listened to the voices from the crowd and looked at their faces: I was in a mob. I was witnessing the power and security of We, the majority, the mass, those who feel they are the Good and the Right.

There, not two yards away, a college professor and a dozen college students were demonstrating for what they apparently believed in—and were doing it in El Paso, Texas—the city I had always found to be so tolerant and easygoing. I suddenly found myself looking across the 2,000 or so people and trying to imagine what it would be like—what it *was* like—to be a minority facing a majority anywhere. What was it like for a group of Negroes to demonstrate for civil rights in the Deep South—who couldn't put down their placards afterward and fade into the anonymity of the streets but had to stay there, ready to take the consequences?

A young man came along with a sandwich sign—a counter-demonstrator. The sign said, "Don't worry, the squirrels will gather them up before winter." The crowd laughed and applauded.

"Give me a gun and I'll go over there and fight myself, you cowards." The Mexican American woman was not slowing down.

A boy in a jacket that had a coiling dragon on the back jumped out of the crowd and shoved a "Win in Viet Nam" sticker in front of one of the marchers. "Read it!" he yelled. The demonstrator, a well-dressed, studious-looking Mexican American young man, just kept walking and looking straight ahead. "Read it, I said . . . read it!"

"Trexler, you're a disgrace to the college. I hope they fire you." Another yell.

Anything the mob wanted to do was okay now. Yell it out—comic, vitriolic—anything was all right as long as you showed you were part of the group. I looked at the smugness of the people in the crowd. I understood then how murder could be done with the approval of a mob, and how the mob could be counted on to protect you. Everyone was brave and swashbuckling inside the womb of a mob.

I looked at Dr. Trexler passing by, his expression unchanging, his mouth set. I realized again that it took guts to be a dissenter.

The marchers kept moving by, solemn-faced and silent, but as I watched them their cause did not seem the important thing anymore. Free love, Theosophy, Disarmament— what they espoused did not matter. What *was* important to me was: could a group of people in this country, regardless of how unpopular their belief, be allowed to present their views in a dignified way without being subjected to abuse? In San Jacinto Plaza, on a mild November afternoon, the answer was a loud and hostile no.

I left before the demonstration was over. I had seen enough. As I walked out of the plaza—listening to the roars turning to steady boos—I wondered how the Colosseum sounded when the Christians were fed to the lions.

Iraq

In January 2003 I wrote a letter to the *El Paso Times* outlining my reservations about the government's push for war in Iraq. My main points were these: (1) The American public, outraged by the 9/11 attack, wanted somebody to vent their anger against. (2) Since the President could not find Osama bin Laden, he adroitly pointed at the world's number two bad guy, Saddam Hussein, and said, "*He's* the threat to our country! We've got to take him out *now!*" (3) But bin Laden's radical fundamentalists were responsible for the 9/11 attack, not Iraq. (4) There were no verifiable connections between al Qaeda and Iraq. (5) If there had been no 9/11 attack we would not be talking about an urgent necessity for war against anyone. (6) We did not need to rush to war now; it was only the President and his advisers who wanted immediate military action.

In early March, as spring break drew closer, and war more imminent, I felt that I needed to take a stand—not just verbally but literally. I made a poster outlining my beliefs, and when school let out at three-thirty I stood across the street from Austin High holding my poster.

It was an exercise in futility, certainly. But parents picking up their kids glanced out their windows to see what the poster said; a few students wandered over to read and gave a thumbs-up and a nod of approval as they walked on. A student who was on the school newspaper staff asked if she could take a picture. I said sure, and the *Austin Pioneer* later ran an article about the one-person, impromptu antiwar demonstration.

Chicanos, Hair,
and Conscientious Objectors

In 1969 Austin High School began to have racial problems. The basically peaceful 1940s and 1950s were definitely over, and Austin High—which up to then had a largely Anglo-American student body—faced serious social changes. The Chamizal boundary settlement between the United States and Mexico in 1964 had resulted in a rearrangement of school boundaries in El Paso. Mexican American students from the south side, some of whom had been scheduled to enter the city's technical school, were now forced to come to the "gringo school" in central El Paso.

They came reluctantly to the brick building with its golden dome, the school they believed would not like them. They were tied emotionally to their neighborhoods near the Rio Grande—near Mexico. They came with a heightened suspiciousness of the Anglo kids from the "good" homes: the so-called Americans.

So Austin High, the highly regarded middle-class, college-oriented WASP school, was the new home for Chicanos who didn't want to be there.

As racial tensions increased, the school administration seemed unwilling or unable to come to grips with the potentially explosive situation. I wrote an article for the *Texas Observer* about what was happening and what I thought needed to be done, but the piece did not further endear me to Austin's largely conservative faculty.

By 1970 hair—its length, the school dress codes concerning it—had become a controversial issue in El Paso ("hair touching a student's collar or extending over his ears is considered disruptive to the educational process"). Lawsuits were filed; male students were kept from classes if their hair was too long.

I wrote letters to the editor of the *El Paso Times* that were critical of the school district's policy. I tried to make the point that the hairstyles of the young, like their clothing styles, were merely that—styles and not threats to the society or the schools.

My positions on social and political matters—Vietnam, dress codes—did not reflect the positions held by most of my colleagues. I could almost hear the pop of neck bones as certain conservative teachers jerked their heads to look sharply the other way when I walked past them in the halls.

In 1972 two senior students, one Anglo and one Mexican American, came to my classroom after school and wanted to know what they should do. They did not believe in the Vietnam War. They did not want to kill Vietnamese, but they also did not want to leave the country and go to Canada or Sweden. They wanted to be classified as conscientious objectors. I knew them well and believed in the genuineness of their concerns. I wrote letters to the local draft board on their behalf, attesting to their sincerity in requesting that they perform alternate humanitarian duties instead of military service.

Both requests were granted.

Requiem for a WASP School
(1970)

They stand in their tall, glassed-in picture frames, looking out from the uncomplicated 1940s to the crowded main hallway of El Paso's Austin High School. Small gold plates beneath the frames give the identifications: Walter Driver, State Champion, Boy's Single Tennis 1940; Billy Pitts, State Championship, Declamation 1942; Robert Goodman, First in State, Slide Rule 1948. Holding their rackets and winners' cups, wearing their double-breasted suits with wide lapels and wide pants that sag around their shoes, they are reminders of the Days That Were: the days of Admiral Nimitz and General Patton and Ernie Pyle; of Glenn Miller and the Andrews Sisters and "Kokomo, Indiana"; of Jarrin' John Kimbrough and Betty Grable and "One Man's Family." They remain there behind glass, representing the Jack Armstrong–Henry Aldrich–Elm Street America that is gone forever.

It is easy, of course, to understand how rich in memories, how painfully nostalgic, these and other hallway pictures are to an old-timer at Austin High. Why, to him the 1940s mean, well, just about everything that was decent and sensible in American life. They mean kids who weren't perfect, of course, but who nonetheless respected rules and obeyed adults and knew how a human being cuts his hair; they mean jukeboxes and soda fountains and hayrides on Saturday night. They mean getting a lump in your throat listening to a glee club sing "The Halls of Ivy" because even if you weren't Ronald Colman standing before a fireplace in college you understood exactly what that kind of song was saying; it was saying that Our Country Was a Grand and Glorious Place and Our Youth Were the Hope of Tomorrow. And such an old-timer only has to turn from the pictures on the wall and gaze about him to feel an even greater sense of pride, and of loss. For can't he look at thirteen showcases full of cups, plaques, statues, medals that have been earned by the hard-working students of Austin over the years? And over there—although no one ever stops to read them anymore—aren't those still the bronzed words of Theodore Roosevelt: "What we have a right to expect of the American boy is that he shall turn out to be a good American man"?

"The American boy," the old-timer can muse: that's the key to the glory that once belonged to Austin, and to our country. And now look who we have filling these sacred halls: Mexicans.

Austin High School—the name is rich with associations for many El Pasoans. Over the past forty years it has been a symbol of quality education, of good students from good homes, of traditions to be proud of. Students in nearby elementary and junior high schools looked forward to their freshman year at Austin with a certain amount of trembling, respect, and awe, for Austin meant everything a high school was supposed to mean: a long, elegant, two-story stone building for unsure freshmen to get lost in; teachers who presided over difficult courses that "prepared you for college"; a Panther football team that everyone could get excited about in the fall; homecoming assemblies and class officers and Daughters of the American Republic essays and clubs and honors and prestige. Austin was the kind of all-around good school that lawyers, architects, businessmen wanted their sons and daughters to attend.

And then it happened. The forties and fifties wandered innocently into the explosive sixties, and Austin High found itself with a problem on its hands: social change. The image of an Anglo-American, college-oriented student body began blurring into the image of a racially mixed, academically varied student body that was more than half Mexican American. A highly regarded middle-class WASP high school was becoming a gathering place for Chicanos.

To understand this change it is necessary to know something about the geography of El Paso and the location of its high schools. Juárez, Mexico, lies south of the Rio Grande from El Paso; thus traditionally the heaviest concentration of Mexican Americans has always been on the south side. Jefferson and Bowie High Schools, located in south El Paso, have for years been made up mainly of Mexican American students. In contrast, El Paso and Austin High Schools, located in the central part of town, have largely had Anglo enrollment along with a scattering of typically middle-class Mexican American students. The newer suburban high schools—Andress, Irvin, Burges, and Coronado—have also had, with the exception of Burges, relatively few Mexican Americans. Technical High School, in the center of town, was changed this year to Technical Center—a school that next year will no longer offer academic courses or a high school diploma. Thus, since regular classes were being phased out, a number of students—largely Mexican Americans from south El Paso wanting to enter "la Tech"—were forced into the halls of Austin High School last September even though they wanted to go elsewhere.

Here they came, the slow-walking girls of the freshman class. They moved along sidewalks toward a building they had always considered "the gringo school on the hill," the snob school with its fancy golden dome, the school that—so rumor had it—didn't really like Mexicans. They came with their dukes up, not willing, in 1969, to let anyone put them down. They ate lunch in groups, they shouted in Spanish at boys from crowded doorways in groups, they waited in groups for whatever action might develop at the nearby Dairy Queen. And they were not Americans, in their own minds: they were Mexicans, they were La Raza. Their ties were to Mexico—its language, its culture, its dress and mannerisms.

They were the first class ever to enter Austin High

expressing openly the attitudes and behavior patterns of a subculture world (and there seems to be little reason for their younger sisters and brothers to be thinking any differently in 1971 and 1972). They were not concerned with their "future," these stubborn, defensive south side girls. Why should they be? They had on their block-heeled shoes; transistor radios were pressed against their ears; their hair was hanging long and black and loose past their shoulders. Their skirts—brief triangles and handkerchiefs of color—revealed a long, mod stretch of legs halfway up the body.

They were like aliens in a hostile territory, not bothering to care about Austin's Most Beautiful Girl (it certainly won't be a Mexican, they told one another) or the Select Scholars list or the "Let's Really Yell It Now, Y'all" that the blond cheerleader was getting red in the face about down on the gym floor. And they didn't care when they were warned during the morning p.a. announcements that they would "seriously jeopardize future freshman assemblies unless their conduct was more in line with what Austin expected of its student body."

They weren't interested in what Austin expected of them any more than they were interested in diagramming sentences or reading *The Odyssey*. They were simply prisoners being held in an Anglo jail and they would continue to stare out sullenly through their granny glasses until the sentence was lifted.

It has long been the custom of school boards to select principals and other administrators from the ranks of coaches. It is not unusual, therefore, that the principal of Austin High is a former football coach; that the coordinator of instruction and guidance—presumed by many to be the successor to the principal when he retires—is an ex-coach also; and that the counselor most influential with the Austin administration is a former basketball coach. (Indeed, Austin is such a sports- and coach-oriented school that teachers in the good graces of the administrators are likely to be addressed by them as "coach." Thus the most unathletic math or government teacher finds himself being called "coach" as he requests an overhead projector or discusses a class load, for *coach* is the official password, the casual sign of camaraderie, the measuring stick of status.)

It is safe to say that the principal and the coordinator love Austin High School, that they consider it to be the core of their life's work. It is also safe to say that both are sincere, intelligent men who are doing their jobs as they see them and who want perhaps more than anything else to keep Austin's image as a Good School from being damaged.

But sincerity, intelligence, and love of school—certainly adequate equipment for administrators during the less complex era of the forties—are not enough to cope with the unsettling seventies. What is also needed is a high degree of flexibility in responding to potentially explosive situations that did not exist thirty years ago; a willingness to understand and trust student leaders who ask for change; and perhaps more than anything else, empathy with persons of minority groups—especially, in El Paso, Mexican Americans.

High school administrations are generally conservative by nature; Austin's administration is perhaps more conservative than most. It thus views hippies, Reies Tijerina, César Chávez, black militants, antiwar demonstrators, college longhairs, etc., with a wholly unfriendly eye. The faculty, however, shares in large part this same conservative view. (Austin's Teacher of the Year for 1969–70, selected by Austin teachers, had a sticker on his car reading "Register Communists, Not Firearms.") Whether the teachers' conservatism is directly related to age is conjectural, but the fact that out of a staff of over one hundred probably less than half are under the age of forty does suggest that the majority of the faculty is far from being attuned to the strident harmonies of today—especially those voiced with a Spanish accent.

During the past year there was mild racial tension— mainly in September when a Chicano walkout was threatened and Mexican and Anglo groups fought several afternoons after school; there was an awareness that the "melting pot" togetherness that Austin had begun priding itself on during the last few years had gradually begun to disappear; there was a feeling among many of the Mexican American students—not just the reluctant freshmen—that they were the Unseen and Ignored Majority as far as honors, offices, awards, etc., were concerned. There was also a grim little war concerning censorship of the student newspaper, the *Pioneer*.

At the beginning of the year an administrative staff member had been assigned the extra duty of censoring the *Pioneer*. (Such censorship by an administrator rather than the journalism teacher was a citywide policy.) In October the administrator censored a letter to the editor by junior journalism student Cecilia Rodriguez. The letter, which dealt honestly with Mexican American experiences and attitudes in typical school situations, was subsequently printed in the University of Texas at El Paso newspaper, the *Prospector*.

In April, a group on the *Pioneer* staff wanted to devote an entire issue to the concerns, problems, and culture of Mexican American high school students. After much discussion—in which a few of the more secure Mexican American students themselves balked at being singled out for special attention ("We're all Americans, aren't we?")—it was agreed that a single page of Mexican American features would be run. When copy was submitted to the administrator, he cut the four lead articles: "Brown

Misery"; "La Huelga," an article about César Chávez and the California farm workers' grape strike; an article on the origin and significance of the term *Chicano*; and "The Race United," an article on the newly formed political party in Texas for Mexican Americans.

It was a typical student-administration conflict. The administrator, in keeping out of the *Pioneer* what he considered to be extremist or inappropriate material, felt, one can be sure, that he was fulfilling his role as censor and was doing what was best for Austin High. What he did also, of course, was frustrate—once again—the efforts of some of the most creative, conscientious, and morally sensitive students at Austin—both Anglo and Mexican American. ("Change this school?" said one depressed student afterward. "Never. You see how much trouble we had getting just one lousy, watered-down page in the *Pioneer*." Another student added: "They say their doors are always open—yet every time you go to see them their minds are always closed. You can see *No* staring at you before you even open your mouth.")

Thus the staff member added another footnote to an already familiar tale: high school administrators ironically helping to create the very college radicals whom they dislike, as well as stimulating the possibilities for an underground press. For the students finally end up believing what they really, at first, do not want to believe: that the administration *doesn't* really care to understand what they are trying to say, *doesn't* realize that times have drastically changed, *doesn't* care about the quality of people's lives if those lives are led by blacks or browns, *doesn't* care to admit to the reality of a world that exists right outside the classroom doors in the streets, on the television sets, in the books available at every drugstore. Such students who try to express their idealism, and fail, simply resign themselves rather bitterly to their high school fate and wait for college—when they feel they can get rid of all their pent-up frustrations in orgies of action.

Thus, at a crucial moment in its history, Austin seems to be maintaining a steady course of drift. Apparently, the official policy is business as usual. Don't rock the boat if you want to be considered a good fellow. And don't stir up any trouble about problems that you feel are mounting—wait and see if they don't go away as they always have in the past.

But what is buried at the heart of the problem? Why *should* Austin teachers sigh at the prospect of their high school being filled with Mexican Americans? Why, really, should Mexican Americans be less academically capable than Anglos? Who is to blame?

The problem is many-rooted and complex, of course. Yet if there is an answer to the question, Who has been at fault, it should be arrived at after considering these points:

1. For too long Mexican Americans have been offered the least and the worst of everything that is available in Texas, from jobs to housing to education to social status. They have been forced to live on the bottom rung of society and adopt the survival rules of what Daniel Moynihan has called the "underclass." They learn at a very early age not to believe in the "better tomorrow" of America's Protestant ethic. They learn not to believe they will get ahead by merely studying hard and saying yes-sir and going by all the rules. They learn not to hope or to save up nickels for a rainy day. They learn not to be open and trusting and optimistic. Indeed, they learn many things that do not help them get A's in government or spelling.

2. A study of underprivileged children, by Norma Radin (condensed in the September–October 1968 issue of *Children*), has this to say about the "hidden curriculum" that is available in middle-class homes but that is generally absent from homes of the disadvantaged: "Shapes, colors, numbers, names of objects, words on signs, etc., are part of the continuous input to the child. . . . Books are read, stories are told, intellectual curiosity is rewarded, and efforts perceived as school-oriented are praised. These activities are not part of the mother's role in the lower-class home." The study also states: "A large fraction of the intelligence of a child is already fixed by the age of five. No amount of environmental change

beyond that point can affect the intellectual capacity to any significant extent."

3. Granting the difficulty of trying to do alone what society as a whole should do, and granting the possibility that some Mexican American children by age five are already too severely handicapped to compete on an equal basis with Anglos, the public school administrators of El Paso should nevertheless be held accountable for failing to implement—years ago—a program of bilingual education for elementary grade Mexican American children. Chances are the school system will not remedy these children's needs until officials decide to give them massive assistance and the highest priority: until they decide that not only the bright Debbies and Bills from middle-class homes have the right to become surgeons and bankers and civil engineers but also the Rogelios and Alicias from south of Paisano Street who have typically grown up not able to read and not seeing much point in learning how to anyway.

The school system must try bold new approaches in order to break the miserable chain of failure that has linked each successive wave of Spanish-speaking students. The traditional methods have not worked, and Head Start—which gets children after the first crucial five years—is simply not enough. Therefore, if the school system does not wish to perpetually deny children from

Spanish-speaking homes a chance at the greatest possible success our society offers, then it must implement programs that will allow a child who speaks no English in the first grade to nevertheless become proficient in writing and reading English in a reasonably short time.

4. The voting public bears part of the blame for school ills. One group generally wants "safe" school board members—those who will go slow—instead of concerned, progressive individuals who understand the need for change. The other group refuses to vote at all: it always lets conservatives have their way at the polls and determine important elections with a few hundred votes.

5. Many nervous parents transfer their children from the inner-city schools to those in the suburbs—leaving the inner-city schools to become, finally, all Mexican American. This happens because the typical middle-class Anglo parent is unwilling to run the risk of having his child receive less than what he conceives to be the best education—that is, the parent refuses to let his child pay the penalty for society's failure to educate Mexican American children so that they are on a par with Anglos. Thus he sends his son to the suburbs—hoping the kid won't get on pot or acid—and leaves such schools as Austin and El Paso High to sink or swim with the many black eyes and brown skins. (Classic example: For many years El Paso High School

was attended by students from the affluent Kern Place and Rim Road sections "on the hill" above the school, as well as by students from modest homes in the flatland below. It was a relatively successful mingling of rich, poor, and middle-class. Then Coronado High School was built in northwest El Paso, and school authorities gave parents the choice of sending their children to Coronado or El Paso High. The Anglo rush toward a lily-white school began and thus El Paso High—finally cut off from the Rim Road and Kern Place areas through obvious gerrymandering—has had its enrollment drop by approximately 1,000 students.)

If school administrators genuinely want to educate students for the lives they will be leading in the seventies and eighties—rather than just keeping them quiet and off the streets—they must provide courses and teachers that are meaningful to both the highly motivated academic students and the indifferent, withdrawn couldn't-care-lessers. They must also determine which teachers do the incredibly difficult job of plunging into their subjects and making them exciting, challenging, alive—and which teachers merely show up for work, "keep order" with a deadening fervor, and then go home again.

And the principals: they should be energetic, widely read men who are conversant with the issues of the times and the problems that face students in their schools. They should be men who are constantly mingling with their students—staying in touch, hearing what they have to say in this era of intense social concern and audacious questioning of the status quo—rather than presiding over their desks in their offices. They should be shirtsleeves-rolled-up administrators of the seventies, moving among students the way Mayor Lindsay moves through the people of New York. They should be courteous, open-minded, contemporary men whom the students feel are on their side—which, of course, they will be if they are successful principals.

The pictures on the wall at Austin High will continue to look out from a simpler time. Whether it was also a better, more just, more democratic—more American—time is still to be decided. If we truly wish to educate everyone and not just an elite—and if we find ways to turn that wish into a reality—then the glory that was yesterday will pale beside the glory of today.

"Requiem for a WASP School" received the 1970 Stanley Walker Award for journalism from the Texas Institute of Letters.

"Will You Hold Me?"

The students, the never-ending flow of students—an average of twenty-five in a class, five classes a day, for forty-eight years. Each name on the roster represented a life, and I was there each day with that name, that life, and then the name and the life moved on, faded from view, replaced by other names, other lives.

—1958, Kingsville. I am teaching an eighth grade class. Clarissa sits near the front: red-haired, a powdering of reddish freckles across her nose. She raises her hand. "Oh, Mr. Bode, could we go on a walk? It's such a nice day." It *was* a nice day, with the smells of the trees and flowers and watered grass coming through the open classroom windows. So my eighth grade students, who had never done such a thing, went for twenty minutes on a "writing walk" down the sidewalks of the school and the neighborhood, each student clutching a pencil and a tablet, looking self-consciously at the mesquites and bougainvillea, trying to see something "important" enough to write about.

—1968, Austin High School. Daryll raises his hand. "Mr. Bode, are you a Communist? My mother says you are."

—2003, Austin High School. Joshua, who is a Jehovah's Witness, has asked if he could come by my room at lunchtime. Of course, I say. He comes in, sits down in the row next to me. I open my sack lunch, and he opens his. He waits a moment, then asks, "Are you saved?"

—1975, Austin High School. Slender, soft-spoken, and very bright, Thomas had sat at the back of the room during his sophomore year, offering well-phrased responses during class and turning in excellent compositions and making his 99s and 100s. He looked out through rimless glasses and kept his own counsel. I decided, finally, that he was gay and did not know what to do about it.

One afternoon the following year I was working late at my desk when Thomas appeared in the doorway and asked if I was busy. I said no and told him to come on in. He sat down and I continued to do paperwork at my desk and nod from time to time as he talked about his junior classes, about the science project he was working on, about a piece he was writing for the school literary magazine. It was obvious that he wanted to talk also about other things but was unable to come directly to the point.

The afternoon light in the windows had grown darker. My end of the building was empty. I could hear through the open classroom door the occasional faint knocking of the custodian's broom far down the hall.

There were stretches of talk, periodic silences.

I got up from my desk, busied myself with getting-ready-to-leave routines.

I pulled down the window shades on the finally dark November afternoon.

I was about to ask Thomas if he needed a ride home when he stood as I walked past his desk.

"Will you hold me?" he asked.

The room was silent. The building was silent. Thomas was standing there, and I had to make a decision.

I held him.

He did not say anything, but finally his shoulders shook and he cried quietly.

He graduated the next year and moved to Montana, where he made jewelry in a crafts shop run by an older man who became his companion.

Music

There were no other adults in the room, but I did not feel isolated. I had the companionship of music. I had Mel Torme, Stan Kenton, Willie Nelson, Jerry Lee Lewis, James Taylor, Stan Getz, the Modern Jazz Quartet, Peggy Lee, the Mamas and the Papas — many more. They kept me company in the vacant after-school hours while I sorted through stacks of papers to take home and got materials ready for the next day's classes.

At the beginning of each school year I brought to my classroom four or five shoeboxes filled with tapes and CDs, a dozen or so LPs, and my cassette player. I stuck the boxes on the bookshelves by the window, checked out from the audiovisual room a serviceable record player. (Oh, that record player: it was definitely an artifact from the Olden Days, always a source of mild curiosity, even head-shaking disbelief among the technologically with-it members of the modern generation.)

It was a comfortable thing to have music and to use music in the daily routines of the classroom — not just having it available in the afternoon as a kind of pleasure I allowed myself as a reward for services rendered, but also using it wherever I could with the class assignments.

When I asked students to write original ballads in sophomore English, I played — in addition to the traditional English ones like "Barbara Allen" — Burl Ives's "The Ballad of Frankie and Johnnie," Jimmy Dean's "Big Bad John," and, naturally, Marty Robbins's "El Paso."

In junior classes when we were reading *The Grapes of Wrath* I played Kris Kristofferson's "Here Comes That Rainbow Again"—based on the scene in which the Okie father and his two barefooted little boys come into a Route 66 café, the father wanting to buy half a loaf of bread with his dime, the boys fascinated by the sight of peppermint sticks behind the glass candy counter. We also listened to Bruce Springsteen's "The Ghost of Tom Joad," based on the famous scene toward the end of the novel when Tom is saying his memorable good-bye to Ma Joad.

But I used music a lot more when I taught creative writing.

"Okay, what do you see?" I would ask, getting the students ready to do a writing assignment. "You're actually not going to see anything, of course, except the front of the room or the back of somebody's head. But as you listen to this piece of music for the next seven or eight minutes, what do the sounds gradually make you see? What scene, what images begin to appear in your mind?" And I would begin the tape of Ravel's "Bolero."

Some students, typically, began to see a scene out of, say, *Lawrence of Arabia*, or stately moving ballet dancers on stage, or warriors gradually emerging from forests— whatever the slow-moving, repetitive, hypnotic sounds seemed to suggest. Other students would continue to sit there and see nothing at all—unable to conceptualize anything that was not in front of them on a TV or movie screen.

Or I would turn out the lights at the beginning of another lesson and say, "Now close your eyes and imagine that you are in a place of darkness—a cave, or a big, abandoned warehouse at night, or maybe the sewers underneath Paris—those tunnels that some of you read about in *Les Misérables*. Wherever you are, whoever you are, write about trying to move through or explore or escape this possibly threatening place of darkness."

The students would open their eyes. I would play the thundering, portentous organ music of Bach's "Tocata and Fugue" as they wrote in semidarkness.

Or I would ask the class what topics poems usually are about. I got the predictable answers: love, nature, sorrow, death, beauty. Then I would say, with studied innocence, "Well, today you are going to have a chance to write on a topic you may not have thought of before." I would turn to the board and with a flourish write in large letters: ROACHES.

("Mis-ter!" a girl or two might say, making a face. I raised my hands in a placating, just-hold-on-a-bit gesture.)

I would tell them—yes, here we go again—to put their heads down on their desks and close their eyes.

"Of course we need to have some suitable 'roach music' to get us in the proper frame of mind." Then I began my little scenario: "It's ten o'clock on a Saturday night, and the humans are gone from the apartment. The kitchen is quiet. Then, one by one, from the cracks in the wall, here come the members of the roach family." I played the opening of Henry Mancini's "Baby Elephant Walk." The Mancini fun-and-games calliope sounds sort of gave the idea. "See them?" I said. "There's Mama Roach" (a poopy-doop noise), "—and Papa Roach" (a kind of muffled thud-thud), "—and Baby Roach" (chirpy tin whistles). "They're coming out of hiding . . .

"Now," I continued, "Leroy Roach and Melissa Roach are beginning to make eyes at each other across a piece of bacon, lettuce, and tomato sandwich, then sort of sliding their feelers suggestively toward one another. It's romance time!" And I played a little of a Mancini chorus singing "The Days of Wine and Roses"—but I quickly shifted the record needle so that what the students heard was "Days of Wine and Roa-ches."

"But," I'd keep on, "a few of the roaches are neighbor-hood wanna-be tough guys who have been hanging around street corners, looking for some roach action." I elaborated a little more on the macho theme, and then from an old LP—trusty record player put to use again—I played the opening from "Kung Fu Fighting," trying to get the class to visualize a Bruce Lee roach high stepping and antennae-kicking his way down the inner-city streets.

And so on. Finally it was their turn—to keep some of

that imagery in mind and write some "roach poems." (And they did: "Romeo Roach and Juliet Junebug," "Harry Roach and the Sorcerer's Meat Loaf.")

Bushy-bearded Roberto was the afternoon custodian for my area of the building, and it soon became obvious that he liked to clean my room because he could count on hearing my music—which, it turned out, was his kind of music—as he pushed his broom between the desks. Roberto had played guitar with a local group on weekends for a long time, and he was still a Doobie Brothers/Glen Campbell/Elton John kind of guy.

Usually at about four o'clock he would give his knock, wait a moment, then open the door a crack and peer in, smiling widely. I would look up from my desk and motion him in.

He had established early on that he was definitely not a hip-hop fan. For him, today's music wasn't music anymore. It had gone wrong decades ago. He had no tolerance for the head-banging noise that came out of the boom boxes of cars cruising past the school in the afternoon. Sinatra and the Rat Pack, the big bands of the 1940s—they were music. The current stuff sucked.

My room, then, was a little island of music sanity for him. As he emptied the wastebasket or gave an obligatory swipe with his cleaning rag at the chalkboard, he was focused on the sounds from the cassette player. "Hey-y-y, ol' Willie!" he chuckled as he listened to a tune from *Red-Headed Stranger*. Or, "You know, I sure miss Jim Croce," he would say as "Time in a Bottle" played. Or, "Mr. Bode, did you get a chance to catch Cher over the weekend at the Special Events Center?"

Roberto was pretty much a C— cleaner of the dust devils gathering in the corners of the room, but let's face it: he was a music appreciator more than a dedicated custodian. The Bee Gees singing "Stayin' Alive" and "You Should Be Dancing" beat emptying out pencil sharpeners any day.

By the time the five-thirty shadows lengthened across the lawn of Austin High, I was usually dragging my heels. I had done the necessary photocopying and set up the slide projector. The movie *A Tale of Two Cities* was ready to go, and I had checked out the set of *Animal Farm* novels from the book room and entered the names of new students in my grade book. I pulled down the window shades and reached for my keys. But it might come to me that hearing, before I left, "Chanson D'Amour" by the Manhattan Transfer or "Georgia on My Mind" by Ray Charles would be a nice way to send me out the door.

Crash Montoya and Ivory John Doe

Each semester as I began my creative writing class, I thought, "It surely won't happen this time." But it always did.

I would ask students to select pen names to use instead of their own names during the semester. I referred to a few well-known writers who, for a variety of reasons, used such pseudonyms: Samuel Clemens (Mark Twain), Eric Blair (George Orwell), William Sidney Porter (O. Henry). I mentioned the English novelist Mary Ann Evans who wrote under the masculine name George Eliot; the Hispanic-sounding Danny Santiago—actually an Anglo writer, Daniel James. And I told them that an El Paso writer, Chester Seltzer, published short stories using the name Amado Muro.

I said that pen names would be a useful way for them to open up, to write honestly about themselves and their personal experiences without worrying how their classmates might react. I emphasized that they would be reading, and responding to—silently, not orally—each other's stories, journals, and poems, but each writer's identity would remain a secret.

I passed out slips of paper and asked each student to write down who he or she would like to "become" for the next few months. I said I didn't care what kind of pen names they selected; they could choose the name of a current celebrity, a comic strip or cartoon character, the name of a girlfriend or boyfriend spelled backward, a wild and nonsensical name—whatever. I wrote on the board a few examples of pen names used by previous students: Acapulco Gold, ZZ Top, Midnight Soldier, Alcatraz, April Showers, Blondie, Ludwig, Terminator, Chronos, Wilson Thornberry.

Each student wrote his or her real name opposite his or her pen name. I collected the slips, put them in an envelope, and went on with the class.

When the school day was over I stared at the envelope for each class and thought my thought: "It won't happen this time." But it did, and that was what seemed remarkable—yea, impossible.

I'm talking about the fact that each semester, as I gazed out at the kids sitting in rows, they seemed to look just like those from the preceding semesters. They dressed the same, used the same slang, talked about the same interests and concerns. Outside the classroom they seemed to watch the same television programs and same videos, listened to the same music, responded to the same influences of advertising.

My continuing question was this: Why shouldn't there be a scattering of Britney Spears pen names, or Shaqs, or some of the new rap or other music icons? Shouldn't those look-alike students with their earrings and stylized ripped-at-the-knee jeans flow like a school of fish to the same cultural heroes—or nonheroes—when they chose their names?

Never. Year after year, semester after semester, I took the

slips out of the envelopes; I wrote the pen names opposite the students' real names in my grade book, and inevitably each identity was different—in some way a personal self-assertion, a private thumbprint.

Mall Rat, Rammstein, Jakou, Pandora Tamerlane, Marshall Mathers, Stitch, The Prophecy, Crash Montoya, Ivory John Doe, Charlie Baltimore, Jodica, Spider Girl, Jada Smith, Kase, Skittle, Straw Kerr, Alex Gal, Lil Kim, Son Gokou, Boogerface, Gary the Rat—one after the other was a declaration of a highly personalized Me in the world of Many. I had no idea what some of the names referred to, but I didn't need to know. The students knew exactly who they wanted to be for a while.

Protected by their pen names, they spilled out their guts, waxed romantic, revealed sexual crises, tried out zany ideas—and did so without fear of being identified by their readers. In a sense—and this was probably what was most important for them—they were being "published" each week when their compositions were passed around the room and comments were written on the attached Comment and Evaluation pages. They had a readership, a constant audience for their work.

It didn't take long before pen-name reputations began to grow. ("Hey, read the next installment by Nine Inch Nails" . . . "Mr. Bode, did Crimson Dragon hand in his stuff this week?" . . . "Dude, check out the second by Sandanista.")

My job, as I saw it, was to offer a variety of topics that students would probably never consider as possibilities for writing. I tried to enable them to "access" themselves—to use current computer slang: to offer them passwords to themselves that would open up the almost limitless possibilities within.

Some, not all, responded positively to the invitation and wrote about old people, dreams and daydreams, heroes, elementary school days, listening to family talk on front porches at night, obsessions and fears, a modern-day Humpty Dumpty, being bored—and how to cure boredom. They wrote fairy tales, letters to God, dialogues with different dialects—plus limericks, acrostics, myths, monologues, fables.

Throughout the semester I tried to make them understand that a blank piece of paper always represented an opportunity: it could bring them emotional release or a chance to explore, safely, areas within them and around them. I stressed that sometimes it was only by the process of writing something down that a person finally came to understand it.

I once told a class that if a Harvard professor were to become interested in them and began to do biographical research, the professor could never learn as much about them as they already knew. They each had a PhD in their own lives.

Other Worlds

William Burroughs wrote that "writers of novels are trying to create a universe in which they have lived or where they would like to live." Each year I tried to take students into the different worlds of novels and plays they might not have entered on their own.

The books were there; the students were there. It was my job to bring them together in such a way that the books were not regarded as just more School Stuff, but as literature that dealt with the serious problems and concerns of life: their lives, their parents' and ancestors' lives.

One of the continuing pleasures of presenting these worlds was reading aloud scenes of a novel or play to a class and having the words of, say, Steinbeck, bring the reader, the author, and the listeners closer together. Until that moment words were often just lifeless black marks on a page—rather meaningless little things to those students who did not care to read very much on their own. But in the classroom, the words now alive, taking on flesh and blood and significance, students could be witnesses to some timeless literary moments.

—In *Of Mice and Men* George is talking to Lennie in the ranch bunkhouse, telling him once again "how it is gonna be" when they finally get their dream place where they can have apricot trees and setter dogs and pigeons flying around the windmill ("an' rabbits, George," Lennie cries out to him). At the end of the novel, their dream world in ruins, George must tell Lennie a final time to "look across the river" as if he can see their dream place there. Then George must put the Luger to Lennie's head and end the dream forever.

— In *A Tale of Two Cities* Sydney Carton stoically maintains his secret love for Lucie Manette. But in the concluding scene, as the heads of the French aristocrats continue to fall at the hands of the revolutionists, he takes his place at the guillotine, ready to sacrifice himself for the woman he loves.

— In *Julius Caesar* Brutus walks back and forth at night at his house, agonizing over the action he must take: kill Caesar, the greatest man in the Roman world, not for what he had done but for what he might do.

There were many more dramatic scenes to present, other books and plays to read. But if I had to pick the one novel that never failed to appeal to sophomore students — the novel that always succeeded in drawing in its readers almost hypnotically — I would have to choose *To Kill a Mockingbird*. It was the most teacher- and reader-friendly novel in the curriculum. I taught it for over thirty years, and with each reading it provided a fresh trip to the 1930s Deep South for the classes to experience.

Atticus, the lawyer father, offered the compelling image of the tolerant good man charting the course between right and wrong for his children. Scout, the child narrator, appealed to students because of her combination of feisty, tomboy ways and an innocence of the grim truths of the adult world. Jem, the older brother, was right beside Scout to protect her as he explored the limits of his young manhood. Bob Ewell remained the prototypical example of southern white trash. Tom Robinson, the black man falsely accused of rape, gave eloquent testimony to the human dignity that should be accorded to everyone everywhere. And Boo Radley, the neighborhood recluse, secretly watched over the lives of Scout and Jem, whom he thought of, protectively, as his own children.

The Atticus Finch family in their small Alabama town was each year a universe that, once visited, was not forgotten.

I suppose I could say that as well about my Austin High family, my Memphis Street universe: once visited, once experienced, they can never be forgotten.

PART THREE

Journals

Sometimes I want to tell people: Visit the desert! Get away from the highways and alfalfa fields. Just walk straight out into the sand and stand a while in a pebbled wash.

Enter at noon in early summer when it is 99 degrees and gnats are in your eyes and nose. Look as far as you can see at the mesquites and greasewood that are blooming, yellow and green. There are no trucks or vans—just the movement of fat summer flies, hummingbirds, bees. Somewhere a quail calls.

As you stand in intense heat you can understand, once again, that you are, indeed, a transient. The desert—the earth—does not know or need you. You do not really matter among mountains, sky, horizons.

———

When I was young I walked past houses at night, and every porch, every street lamp, every window was a mystery to explore, a truth to behold.

I still spend my time walking the way others spend their time breathing or shopping or watching television. Each afternoon, each night I am out on a sidewalk—looking at someone's backyard laundry, nodding at a dog on a chain. The streets of El Paso are my living room; the desert is my home.

———

As I leave the Upper Valley grocery store, a man sits in his old Chevrolet truck, a carry-out boy whistles as he walks back toward the supermarket entrance, a tumbleweed rolls against a faded blue letter box. It is an ordinary moment on an ordinary late afternoon—certainly not everyone's notion of paradise—and it suits me fine. It is just plain old everyday reality, but to me reality is always italicized; it exists in dramatic 3-D.

I could look at paintings in the Louvre and they would not have a greater impact on me than the sight of the tired workman sitting in his Chevy truck, eating Fritos.

Glories of heaven? They can wait. I take my ecstasies from dusty weeds, cedar posts, worn khaki pants.

—

Existence: The presence of all that is, or the awareness of all that is.

Existence: We flirt with the word, assume we know it, understand it, accept it.

Existence: We are "in" it daily—or "have" it—but what do we ever know of it, really?

I can say, "An elm leaf exists; it has existence." I can say this even as I am assuming, with excusable human hubris, that it does not exist in the same way that I exist. I exist, well, *more*, for I am aware of the elm leaf and assume it is not aware of me. I encompass it, whereas it does not encompass me.

As a human, I am aware of, conscious of, a significant amount. Yet I confess I know nothing, really, about myself or the nature of things: of existence. I know no more about the world than the elm leaf does. Existence eludes me.

I am less sure of things today than I was at ten, at twenty. Each year that I live decreases—radically—my sense of assurance and understanding. I stare at raw existence and can say I know nothing about it. And those things that once seemed simple, or obvious, or certain now seem infinitely elusive and complex—beyond human understanding.

—

Consider the human task. Through the narrow passageway of our life we must let the entire universe pass through.

—

A person always moves among monstrous unknowns. His life is like a hidden lake—seeping, obeying unfelt gravities, going steadily to other places.

—

Consider this person: Let's say he has traveled the world over—land and sea, Capri and Rio, Luxembourg and Patagonia. He has searched and wandered and lived an envied life but has never been satisfied, never been at peace.

Then one day he stops at a bare place of rocks: a crag and a cave. He says, defiantly, *This is mine*. And he stops there and builds a hut and feeds the gulls and plants a row of seeds—and smiles.

What would you say he has been looking for, and what would you say he has found?

———

In a universe of billions—billions of everything—what is the value of any one: one life, one consciousness?

I look around, look back, look ahead, and the billions are lining the horizons. All I see is the never-ending, mind-blowing patterns that will relentlessly produce a billion eggs to hatch, a billion stars to glow.

———

Life is as random and remarkable as a dimple.

———

It's as though thoughts are physical things, having weight, and in order to think them one needs a lot of vacant space in his body so they can rattle around.

Let's say you are looking at a stone wall or a man's face. First you take that sight and bring it within your body and let it change itself into thought. Then this wall or face begins to float through your mind and body, attaching itself to associations that lend it depth. Finally, after it roams within you for an hour or a decade or a lifetime, you may want to release that face or wall in the form of words.

So you get a pencil and you try to let the image recreate itself on paper: you let it rejoin life not only with its original fullness and vitality but also with something else—that mysterious and subtle warp that can only come from the touch of a human personality.

———

I owe my life to

My kidneys: If they had hands, I would shake them.

My heart: If I could reach it, I would pat, gratefully, its pulsing head.

My entire body: If it could see me, I would bow to it daily, thanking it for my life.

———

My son was sleeping late that summer morning. He lay in his white jockey shorts next to the open window of his bedroom. His back was brown from swimming; his skin was smooth in the morning light.

He had no hair yet underneath his arms. He would soon be twelve.

As I looked at Byron from the doorway I knew I loved him in the same effortless way that the curtains moved in the window. Yet I wondered if the day would come when such loving would not be enough: when the reality of loving would somehow be insufficient to the strange new reality of my son as a man.

———

I had wandered into the El Paso Centennial Museum at the University of Texas at El Paso and found myself staring at a wall. On it was painted a pictorial chart of the earth's geologic history. Other museum visitors came by, glanced at the colorful depictions of plants and animals, and drifted on. But I was transfixed. I couldn't move.

At the bottom of the mural were the Proterozoic and Archeozoic eras. That section was without any representations because it was a time of "larval life" that left no record of itself. No fossils marked the stay of those first spores and invertebrates.

I gazed at the rectangle that, the words to the side told me, represented a time period that was over 4,000,000,000 years old. Now there was a nice, round figure. I mulled it over, trying to get a handle on what the earth could have been like 4,000,000,000 years ago. I shrugged, admitting helplessness in grasping the concept of billions, and moved upward.

No human folks there, either—just a lot of very blue water and some wiggly aquatics as painted by S. Lopes, the artist. No Baptists around, no Muslims; no Immanuel Kant; just fishes and amphibians and reptiles and gymnosperms. The coal beds had started; Niagara Falls was cutting its way through Silurian rock; the caverns of Carlsbad were being hollowed out. Lung fish were creeping landward.

I kept scanning upward—millions of years passing with every inch. Finally, there they were: the dinosaurs, waiting to rise out of the ferns midway through the chart and claim their piece of evolutionary action. They began in the Mesozoic era along with birds and grasses and flowering plants. Then they died out, too, 140 million years ago.

I reached the top of the chart, and there we were at last: we-the-people, the creatures of consciousness. We were a rather hairy-looking lot, of course, but we had made it—a few billion years late to the Creation Party but nevertheless upright and striding cross the African savannas as if we belonged.

That chart stayed with me over the years, resurfacing in my mind for a variety of reasons. Mainly I think of it when I consider churches, or rather churchgoers, who often seem to ignore the God of evolution and focus only on the God of the narrow top slice of the chart—the God of humankind. It is as if they acknowledge that God created the world a long time ago—yes, of course, certainly—but He only got interested in things when nomadic tribes in the Middle East caught His attention a few thousand years ago.

To me, the God contained in churches, synagogues, and mosques is a God reduced—shrunk to fit human frailties and human needs. To me, a God who would truly be a God is not denominational, is not shaped to the fashion of religious dogma, but would be the Creator of the whole incomprehensibly long process of life. He would be the God of amoebas and mosses long before He became a God of Aaron and Moses. But what such a Creator wanted—what His will was, what was on His mind during all those billions and millions of Archeozoic, Paleozoic, Mesozoic, and early Cenozoic days, when the earth was silently turning in space and humanless—no one can ever presume to know.

———

Spring is childhood and innocence and the gleam of a white plate on an oilcloth-covered table. It is grass shining in a vacant lot at nine in the morning. Spring is when there is no future and there is no past—only tree shadows along a creek, sky above your head.

Spring is the earth's glory written in green, heralded by birds, carried by breezes to every porch and through every window.

Spring—untouched by memories, unburdened by a past—is the first time, the only time, the fresh and clear and timeless time. Spring makes us remember—if we had forgotten—how much it is like a tenderness, like a love.

———

I have tried to write as if I were describing what ordinary things are like to someone—maybe a Martian—who has no idea what earthly life is all about: what a day is, how an afternoon feels. That's the key: getting the ordinary down on paper but in such a way that the ordinary has the specialness, the haunting, elusive timelessness of life itself.

———

We seldom see the shadow of our mortality that always walks beside us. If we happen to glance over our shoulder, we just see another shadowless midday.

———

For me it was right to look at weeds along a canal on Sunday morning while others held their hymnals in church. I felt right at home consulting my text of land and sky.

———

Does anyone know how to live? Being able to pass the days with a certain amount of grace and self-satisfaction—is that the same as learning how to live?

Can anyone actually desire to live tranquilly—to have happiness as a goal—without immediately being eaten up by guilt? With the problems of the world that face us, can one legitimately focus his energies on finding the best way to live at peace with himself?

Which is more significant, the Guadalupe River in the hill country or a war zone, a picnic in the Big Bend or unrelieved poverty in Sudan? Should the realities of society take precedence over the realities of nature? What are the real priorities of any age?

If the problems of living unbalance a person so completely that he can no longer juggle commitments to himself and to others, must he make a choice? Citizen or self? Involvement or isolation? What if private concerns keep being battered down by the news of the day? Will journalism finally replace art?

Become involved! Act! Believe in the plight of your fellow man: yes!

But everyone cannot be continuously involved with his fellow man. Isn't it possible—even natural—to have, without developing a paralyzing sense of guilt, a personal life with personal goals and tastes and desires that have no specific reference to the needs of others? Aren't the choices made because of one's temperament legitimate ones?

Let Camus have a word here: "A man's work is nothing but this slow trek to rediscover, through the detours of art, those two or three great and simple images in whose presence his heart first opened."

Can I remain true to my own "great and simple images" in the face of an Islamic jihad?

Will we be driven to our graves by a sense of overwhelming despair, by being aware, through the modern magic of instant, total, continuous communication, of what every other human on earth is in need of, is suffering from? Should private, personal goals be altered—jettisoned—as we become, more and more, a world community? As we increase our knowledge of and thus our sense of responsibility for every other human—indeed, truly become our brother's keeper—will there evolve a new human trait: permanent discontent? Will our new quest be a perfect earth, a heaven on earth for everyone? Will there be no privateness and no rest until all mankind is well fed, well clothed, well housed, well educated?

In the name of a perfect world society, will we become soldiers in the army of change? Shall everyone band together by the chanting millions in order to bring social reforms and social justice to the last outposts of the world—removing, as we go, all the human quirks of personality and self, all the old human idiosyncracies, prejudices, pleasures, loves?

———

She and I, 1957: I was twenty-six and she was twenty-five on a day of deep closeness, the day of the first fall breeze; the day of coffee in a thermos on the car seat between us and photographs taken along hot, still, narrow-laned roads. A day of oak-shaded filling stations in small, quiet, hill country towns; a day of not quite full-blooming love but almost; a day of words easily summoned and of a mutual ease; a day of miles driven in pleasing silences and pleasing talk. A day of gradually coming night and then of the September night itself, of a boundless, unhurried, sanctioning darkness: a night almost hidden from itself in blackness, almost purposefully discreet. A night, as we sat parked among trees, that seemed to say there is no place but this, no bodies but yours.

———

I sat in the house, waiting for the phone to ring me the bad news.

The windows rattled in their slots as the wild gusts swept across the yard. The fireplace chimney sucked at the wind and moaned.

As I stared outside, the limbs of the elm trees jerked clumsily like the heads of panicked horses. Sheets on the backyard clothesline rose and spread and tunneled as though gasping for breath.

Every once in a while the wind calmed, and I could hear again from across the room the slow ticking of the mantel clock as it measured out the moments of the universe.

———

The older we get, the more daily routines take the sparkle from our lives. Dutifulness dulls us, our sensitivities and perceptions. We go through the practiced motions of our jobs, and in doing so we lose touch with the vitality we had when we were new on the job, tentative, slightly off balance. We once had to find our way through unfamiliar territory, but now we know the ropes; we are old hands. As we look about at the framework of our Eight-to-Five, we see pretty much what we saw the day before—and we are lulled into thinking that this is good news, that being knowledgeable is a fair substitute for enthusiasm or joy. We have, without really knowing it, become resistant to change. We hide behind the protective shield of our gray expertise because it gives us a feeling of control and security, a false sense of mastery over life.

That is why a drastic change in the weather tends to perk people up: it gives us back the sense of being freshly involved in the drama of living. Let the winter winds bring in a bitter, Arctic storm. We gripe and complain, of course, but secretly we are exhilarated by the marvel of it all: the slippery, icy roads, the bluster and fluster of people-against-the-elements. Forgotten yearnings reappear, and we are willing again to surrender ourselves to chance, to physical challenge—perhaps even to discomfort or disaster. We gladly bury our everyday lives beneath a foot of new snow.

———

Every week for years I would swing through downtown El Paso on my way home from work and drive across the Santa Fe bridge into Juárez. I parked near the Florida Club and got in an hour's worth of walking. (This was in the 1960s and 70s when traffic and parking were not a problem. It was easy crossing, easy returning.) I was not a tourist, not a consumer. I was just there to scratch my particular kind of itch: the compulsive desire of the observer to observe.

I gravitated toward the side streets the way other people are attracted to indirect lighting and shag rugs. Mariscal Street on a September day: up above, half-a-skyful of clouds; down below, skinny dogs and dirty-bellied children in diapers sitting in doorways. Along the canal, flowing with muddy water from New Mexico, weeping willows luxuriated next to broken, abandoned adobe buildings. Inside the White Lake Bar prostitutes read comic books in the dim light. Outside on a ledge, pigeons investigated their feathers. Thunder rolled across the five o'clock sky.

Juárez, Mexico: not like Kerrville, Texas, not even like El Paso. I was there as an outsider, but I felt as much at home walking the broken sidewalks as in any place I had ever known.

———

I suppose I am a modern sort of person if I know that I am made, amazingly, of atoms, which, amazingly, are primarily empty space. I have no idea what I am saying when I say it, but, yes, I suppose I am primarily empty space.

There is much more about living the modern life that I do not understand. I do not know how memory works, or how the present moment disappears so seamlessly into the past.

I think, but I haven't any idea how I do it.

I don't believe anyone has figured out yet what is mind and what is brain and how they differ, if they do.

I do not understand emotions. A person has one body, one set of bones and flesh, yet if that body gets a certain kind of signal the throat tightens and tears well up and flow. If it gets another signal then anger—like a hibernating bear suddenly awakened—comes roaring forth. If it gets still another signal here comes sadness, surging up and over the person like fog swirling in from the sea. Yet before the signals come the person cannot feel them, does not know they are there: the fog, the bear, the tears.

I walk, I eat, I sleep, I carry on conversations—and the "I" that does this, I am told, is really not the all-controlling "I" that I seem to be but a swirling commotion of acids and proteins and electrical firings. These unseen parts are actually the "I" that I presume myself to be.

Let's face it: I am cells.

They let me feel pleasure; they form my thoughts. They silently grow my hair, my fingernails. They die within me constantly and are replaced, and I never get to know them.

I am pretty much like the person who gets into his car, turns on the ignition, and complacently drives away without the slightest idea of how the engine works: the driver being driven.

———

Style is simply the shape a writer's personality takes after he has been forced to twist about, here and there, trying to find the most comfortable position in which to survive.

———

There are talkers of words and writers of words. Talkers can be writers, too, of course, but generally they are not. A talker achieves release only if there is a listener being impressed by his words. He does not have that same opportunity for ego satisfaction when he faces paper; he is not at all sure that he can impress it. The needs and uncertainties that he buries beneath the steady sound of his own voice are uncomfortably loud in his ears as he faces the stony indifference of an empty page.

———

I need acres of time to set down, memory by memory, the meaningfulness of who I am: to record the snail slick of my passing, the briefly charged intimacies of my days, the residues of my private fires.

———

I woke once from a night of dreaming, and in that brief, half-lit moment I watched myself change gears from sleeping to waking. It seemed as though my body were rising from where it had lain overnight. I could see the outline the body left in the clay of my dreams. There were two halves of me: the rising-body half that was my recognizable self, the part I had always called me; and its counterpart in the clay, a waiting sunken-mold half into which the body recessed at night to become complete.

For an intense split second I glimpsed a forbidden sight: the image of one's self in its secret wholeness and intimacy. It was like looking into a mirror and seeing through to the other side.

———

As Mark Twain, Hemingway, Steinbeck, and others have proved so clearly, it is the simple telling about a thing that best conveys reality. But certain experiences in life seem to defy simple, straightforward telling. Trying to describe them is like a lover wanting to unite perfectly with the one he loves: such an immersion of self, such a total possession of Otherness, is impossible. It is out of this inability to reveal to a reader what they have perceived that writers despair.

Indeed, from my earliest fumbling with words until now my whole purpose in writing has been not merely to describe but to see through an experience, to present it, always, as phenomenon, and then have words become the thing itself rather than words about it.

———

Being divorced is listening to "Moon River" on Muzak as you eat a sandwich by yourself in a K-Bob's restaurant at seven-fifteen on a Friday night.

———

To see the world anew you must have new eyes. You must look at an object that you have noticed a thousand times before, but now, when you look at it, you see it with its familiarity erased. It is still the same real object, the same chair or window, in the same real world—an object you long ago assumed you had nothing more to learn about—but now you are seeing it with intensity, with an unprejudiced clarity, as if it is a strange new thing about which you have no knowledge. You are seeing the way children first see, or those psychedelic users who, on LSD, saw reality through their spaced-out doors of perception.

———

To see with new eyes is to look around, and where another might see a familiar morning, you are astonished to see creation itself emblazoned on the air.

———

Since I believe in evolution, I have to ask, Where did the soul (if it exists)—the human soul—come from? Surely it had to evolve just as the brain and lungs and ankle bones did—from a less complex form. And if it did, why do people believe that only humans ended up with souls and not worms, horses, and parakeets? A soul would not suddenly materialize out of thin air toward the end of the evolutionary process, announcing to mankind, "Hey, guys, here I am, finally, and I'm just for you!"

(Was there, indeed, a primitive, underdeveloped precursor of the later, more fully developed soul: Soul Lite?)

———

At noon I see a rock sitting within its own shadow. If it could speak and comment upon its state, perhaps it would say: I have substance, and I cast a shadow. I'm okay.

In the glaring afternoon of my life I lack that substance, that depth and weight. I am not okay; I am not content. I have somehow lost my shadow.

———

I cannot shake loose from my terrible focus of recent years. I stare, hypnotized, into that miniscule place where life begins: where human sperm meets egg. Religion, art, philosophy, politics—what grand but secondary irrelevancies these seem to be beside the basics of genes and chromosomes. All mystery is there; all is contained, all is foretold for humans in that monumentally small space.

The liverspots that will appear on the hand of a fifty-year-old man are there, before birth, in the microscopic dot of his life. The billions of cells in his brain, the hairs in his nose, the network of veins and arteries and capillaries, the enzymes and lymph nodes and fingernails and ten separate toes are there, in the human egg no larger than a pencil dot.

I cannot function. I walk around dot-dazzled, dot-dazed.

———

I cannot stop focusing on the ordinary and the everyday because the ordinary is the essence of life's mysteriousness.

———

The meaning of human experience is beyond the capacity of humans to understand.

———

I could spend a lifetime just trying to understand the migration of birds, the incredibleness of the eye.

———

I sat at the bar of the Mexican Elder Restaurant, staring at a glass half-filled with rum-and-Coke. Children in Third World countries were dying of disease and malnutrition, the Middle East was poised on the edge of another war, and the piano player behind me was playing "Blue Moon." It was a typical late-afternoon moment in the drama of daily living, a familiar mixture of misery and ecstasy, heartache and ice cream.

I sat there, paralyzed by polarities but trying, once again, to get a grip on things. For most of my adult life I had been struggling to achieve some kind of comfortable stance, a proper position from which I could finally balance the insoluble contraries in life and announce, if not to the world then to myself: This I believe.

I looked at the piano player in his dim cave behind the piano. Night after night he sat there, summoning up hundreds of tunes—ballads of the 1930s through the 70s— each a pleasure to hear, each played with graceful flourishes and style. He played for the customer, yes, but he seemed to be playing mainly for his own satisfaction.

Taking my cue from the piano player, I ordered another rum-and-Coke, pulled out a notepad, and began to declare some of my own convictions of a sort. I believed, I wrote, in the following:

Sherwood Anderson. I would like to have stood with him a while in the quiet, after-dark streets of *Winesburg*, listening to the strange beauties of lives being lived behind the harness shop, in the mercantile store. I would like to have sunk into the darkness of small, turn-of-the-century Ohio towns and then walked out country lanes into Anderson's fictional landscape.

Ranch women in central Texas. I can see such a woman in coat, curlers, and scarf on a winter day. It is noon, and she is closing a gate on a farm-to-market highway. She has driven down the gravel road from her ranch house to the highway, has gotten the mail, and is now ready to get back inside her pickup. She turns from the gate toward her truck, looks at a car driving past, recognizes the driver as a neighbor, and smiles and waves. Written in the wrinkles of her soft, round, once pretty face is a testimony: an exquisite blur of lines that reveals the mysterious process of her human living and her gradual aging.

A pair of lovers at Port Aransas. I remember watching them standing together on the shore — the full-shouldered, strong-legged man, the trim-bodied woman. They looked at each other, smiled, then waded slowly into the easy waves, hand in hand, as the seagulls coasted above them, as the earth and the Gulf stood still, as the coastal sky blazed down.

Bulverde, in the hill country north of San Antonio. At five in the afternoon I would go there and stand among the fields and fences. At sundown it was my place of intimate stillness. Branches of oak trees would nod a little in the mild December breeze; shadows stretched across a field. Dogs barked on a farm nearby.

To a casual observer it was just another roadside and another end of day — with another farmer's house up the slope, another frost-browned hayfield caught in the dying sun. But to me creation itself was breathing soundlessly in the line of trees along the creek, in the flat gray rocks of the crumbling rock fence, in the grass along the road. The moment, so deceptively ordinary, seemed to be the closest I could ever get to experiencing something mystical.

It was as if I stood on one side of an invisible line, and just across it—unperceivable by human senses—lay the Other World, the Other Reality.

I listened, trying to hear the sound of eternity in the early night hum of insects along the creek.

I remember the first time I sat down and tried to think. It was not easy. I decided that I had never done any genuine thinking and that what I had always called thinking was probably something else: talking or listening or reading or daydreaming or just being intent on some task or other. I had been mentally occupied, sure, but I had probably never, ever thought.

So I sat in a chair by the front room window and decided I would force myself to think, and while the thinking was going on I would sort of stand outside myself and monitor the process—check to see if I was getting it right or not.

Now by thinking I think I meant stirring up something original. In college I had read about famous people who were not just scientists and writers and doctors and mathematicians but who were also thinkers: they seemed to have flashbulbs of new ideas popping constantly in their heads.

But as I sat there in my chair on that summer morning, the terrible thing was I couldn't determine what my mind was doing. It certainly wasn't churning out any new concepts. My head seemed totally vacant. I sat with my arms folded, and all I could focus on was the hum of the refrigerator and the sound of an ambulance somewhere on the freeway. I closed my eyes and tried to form, at a midpoint between them, an image of the sun. (That was a technique I had heard about from a fellow who had gone to a guru in Taos: close your eyes, let a little sun-like disc materialize in front of you, and focus on it until you more or less lose yourself in it.) I stared ahead with tightly closed eyes and got a kind of spiderweb effect with a big black blob in the center but nothing else.

I sat there for half an hour or so. I couldn't make a sun. I couldn't by force of will cause any vital, original thoughts to rise up from my subconscious like nice big pastel-colored balloons. I kept listening to the hum of the refrigerator and the outside sound of birds—getting more and more depressed about the whole business.

Finally I got up and made a pot of coffee, halfway resigned to the fact that I would just have to go through life without gracing the world with a single original thought.

———

Life was the rock wall beside the Circle K convenience store at seven-fifteen on a Tuesday night. I sat in my car, looking at a homeless man slumped against the wall and staring past an empty Budweiser can into his worn-out shoes.

Life was the seven-fifteen glare of lights in front of the Circle K as a young woman wearing a tight black dress and smoking a cigarette got a bag of ice from the metal ice box by the front windows. She put it into the back seat of her Camaro, and then, after surveying the street, the alleyway, the night sky, she hoisted herself and her thin legs and her black dress and her firmly lipped cigarette into her car and roared away.

Life was the last remaining afterglow of the April afternoon and the sound of distant dogs and the talk of children from nearby homes as they walked in twos and threes into the Circle K to buy their Cheetos and milk and bread.

Life was the wildly scrawled and indecipherable graffiti that I did not try to translate from the rock wall as I finally drove away from the Circle K and got on I-10 and looked west at the dark cloud formations that were like other, equally indecipherable messages looming against the sky.

Life was driving home on the freeway while sleek little capsules of cars zipped past me with self-assured maneuverings—their paired rear lights becoming red cigarette glows in the darkness ahead.

Life was gripping the wheel—half expecting one of the cement blocks to sail off the back of the flatbed truck just ahead and crash through my windshield.

Life was driving home as empty of certainties as the homeless man was, staring into his shoes.

———

In the early morning, on my way to work, I walked toward my car parked in its customary place. I saw it, the yard, the street—and everything was unreal. It looked real, of course, and I was once again supposed to take for granted that it was real. That ordinary scene—car-and-street-and-yard—was what we have always called life: the fixed and substantial continuation of the familiarity of yesterday.

But standing beside the car door I was overwhelmed by a sense of transience—of other realities profoundly significant yet unseen, unknowable; of the ongoing process of death and dying that had placed an invisible film over the yard, the water hose, the cat on the porch. All deaths to come, all deaths of the past hung in the sunshine like a shroud, like a sheet that is stretched over the household furniture of the deceased.

———

Sometimes the urge to write is simply the desire to penetrate the mystery of a moment that will not fade away.

I have reached the corner of the vacant lot that lies across the street from my Kerrville home. I am ten or eleven years old, and I have walked the three blocks from Tivy Elementary School. It is noon on a school day, in spring, and once again I am about to cross unpaved Gilmer Street and open the front gate and walk under the oak trees onto our front porch. I am going home to eat dinner.

That's all: I am paused on the path beside the familiar vacant lot with the warm smell of weeds and spring flowers rising up around me and the calling of the doves in the trees of the vacant lot and the sound of a car here and there on the nearby streets and the sun shining down on all the neighborhood houses.

It is like a "Rosebud" moment from *Citizen Kane*—a brief pause under a hill country sky that fuses security, innocence, and awareness of sensory pleasures in such a way that, together, represent my childhood.

———

I don't think we have a real sense of what humans are up to—what we are doing in our lives. We can't even get a grip on the ordinary concepts of present and past.

At six-thirty on a Wednesday night I was sitting in a downtown café. I had started reading the science section of *Newsweek* and dipping tostada chips into the chile sauce as I waited for my Mexican plate. As I reached again toward the dish, I found myself remembering, with a depth of awareness and feeling that surprised me, a past time and place.

I went ahead and ate my tostada, but I stared beyond

the pages of the magazine into a vague middle distance. Why remember, just then—I wondered—that time, that place, an unimportant late afternoon in 1983 when I had been sitting at a back table in a cowboy bar and grill in Bandera, Texas?

That insignificant moment had been swimming in the strange chemical sea of my unconscious, and then, for no apparent reason, had reappeared before me like a sporting porpoise.

What exactly is a memory? How do we "experience" experience and how do we process it? Does the present actually include the past? If so, why should past be called "past"—be differentiated from "present"—if the present includes it?

The waitress set my Mexican plate before me, and I thought, "I am eating an enchilada and considering a time in the future when—waiting in my car at a stoplight in Durango, Colorado—I will suddenly remember a Mexican plate on a Wednesday night in El Paso . . ."

———

The last day:

I woke up and lay listening through the bedroom window to the outside sounds of Saturday morning: dogs barking, cars passing, a white-winged dove calling from his perch on the roof. Another weekend stretched before me. In a moment I would get up, make coffee, read the paper, then stand at the kitchen window with a second cup of coffee and look out across the backyard. I would—

Then the thought struck me: What if this were it? What if—and I indulged myself, in that long, just awake, still sluggish state, to construct the scenario. What if, right now, a stranger in a long black coat strode into the room, thrust a legal-looking paper toward me and said, "That's it, mister. Here's your notice of cancellation. Life's over for you. By midnight you're history," and then left as peremptorily as he had come?

I had to work at the idea a bit, had to force myself to suspend reality and try to summon the energy to legitimize this game I had idly begun to play. It was like pulling a heavy weight close to me from far away, but I did it. I lay there trying to will myself to accept the new blunt fact: this sunny El Paso morning, this inauspicious date on the calendar, had been transformed into a day without parallel in my life, one for which there was no preparation, no warning. I had awakened to another ordinary day in my life, but now—without fanfare, without drama—that life was over. In the next hour I would be experiencing my last shave, my last time to bend over and put on my socks. Later in the day would be the last time to reach into the mailbox, to see the sun above the ten o'clock trees.

I looked at my watch, remembered that I had to take the dog to the vet. I did not have any more time to loll around in bed and play games.

I got up and headed toward the bathroom. I had a busy day ahead of me.

———

I think there is a certain temperament that responds strongly, continuously, to the aesthetics of the earth—of sunlight and trees, of doves in flight and sage in bloom, of desert rains, of the smells of mountain juniper and pine. I think that such persons, if they happen to be writers, can never quite separate the urge to write from their over-whelming passion for things of the land. This deep, rapturous awareness of the beauties of the natural world can never be satisfactorily put down in words, but they—I— keep trying.

———

When I was young I assumed that writers were not only different from me but also somehow different from anyone I could ever possibly know. I thought writers did writing because they lived in New York or Paris or were geniuses whose words rolled out like silk from a spider's belly.

It was a hard lesson to learn: writing was what a person did because to him life lacked reality until it could be shaped again in the form of words on paper. A writer was a person who, for one reason or another, had an overriding interest in paying close attention to who he was and what was happening to him; a writer's life—his material—was no more exotic or significant than my own.

———

I had gone to use the restroom at a café. As I stood at the urinal, waiting for the kindness of gravity and sphincter muscles, I happened to glance at my right hand resting against the flushing knob of the urinal. I noticed first the flaky and chapped skin; then I stared at the liver spots. My God, my hand, I thought in dismay. It looks . . . gross, to use a teenager's term.

I stood there, bemused. I had been going about my life, paying no attention to the fact that splotches had been growing across the back of my hands the way cedar trees gradually fill up an unproductive and deserted hill country pasture. My mortality had been displaying its telltale message, like little clusters of brown neon signs, to everyone except me.

———

I could have worshipped the land yesterday. It was late afternoon, and I was standing by the Montoya canal among salt cedars and the whirring calls of redwing blackbirds. The canal water was carrying its quiet brown message of rebirth beneath the cottonwoods and elms. The trees along the canal were on parade, standing in a spring salute to the earth. Phalanxes of Caesar's soldiers never presented to Rome a more celebratory moment — such a green-leafed tribute.

—

A writer must lift a thing out of the steaming jungle of experience and place it on the high, dry plateau of art.

—

The universe "does not know we are here." Thornton Wilder said it, and I believe it. But we all desperately want it not to be true. We want to feel as much at home among the planets and stars as we do in our backyards.

—

For a long while my way of looking at the physical world — my personal slant on reality — had been narrowing, deepening, intensifying. Finally, almost on a single day, I reached the point where I no longer saw objects as they actually were — that is, the outer aspect of them. Somehow my vision had become focused, like an X-ray beam, on the inner processes by which the objects had been created.

Since I was no longer able to "see" in the old way and was befuddled by the new reality, I could no longer even consider writing. My writing urge, like that of a painter's, had always been primarily based on the desire to capture the lovely surfaces of the earth — and suddenly the surfaces had disappeared. All I saw was a proliferation of cells: the raw forces of creation. I felt overwhelmed. Write? Of course not. What a pale and feeble thing a word was in comparison to a single blade of grass, product of the enormous invisible energy that had made it appear out of nothingness.

The more I thought of all that people took for granted—glanced at, then turned away from, assuming that they had "seen" and understood—the more paralyzed I became. I kept thinking, Each human baby, born complete within its skin, is a phenomenon beyond comprehension, more amazing than the Milky Way. Each created anything—cricket, weed, Sequoia, dinosaur—is beyond explanation, but here we are, by the millions, acting as if miracles are events that happened in Olden Times instead of within our bodies, our lives, our surroundings, every instant of every day.

This intensity of focus and thought went on for months, and I had to deal with it as best I could. Gradually, as if getting over a long illness, I began to regain my normal sight. I could look once more at a tree and see it as a tree and not as the incredible repository of uncountable, unseen cells, an embodiment of a miraculousness beyond my understanding. I could simply enjoy it again as an elm, a familiar place of shade.

I had strayed into a strange land where humans cannot remain too long if we do not want to lose our moorings. I had looked for a while in a way that humans are not equipped to look and survive. I had tried to stare into the fires of creation as I might have stared into the sun, and I was nearly blinded.

———

I am neither musician nor mathematician, but I believe this is true: a mountain stream in the Black Range of western New Mexico, with afternoon sunlight playing on the smooth round rocks at the bottom of the stream, on the sand granules, on the dark-brown fallen leaves, can offer a satisfaction equal to that provided by a stunningly complicated algebraic equation or a Mozart sonata.

———

Little things please me—like the way the traffic flows one-way on Yandell Street into downtown in the late afternoon. After work I drive past the small red brick homes and look out at the old Mexican American men watering their patches of yard. It is like visiting with them a bit— sort of neighborly—as I coast toward the center of town and the outline of the mountains that lie beyond it like a stage cutout. There is no monotonous, after work stop-and-start on Yandell; it is like being part of a smooth surf rolling in to shore.

Sometimes I park and sit for a while in the central plaza. It is as if I am in the living room with my own family— except it is my *human* family there on the benches. We sit with our newspapers and packages among the pigeons and mulberry trees while children play tag by the central pond. We are peaceful. Another El Paso day has been sunlit and satisfying.

———

People who live their lives divorced from the glories and beauties they first glimpsed in childhood grow jaded and sour, feeling that something vital is lacking. They take vacations to get in touch again with animals and seashore, mountains and grassy land, to feel somewhat small again in the grand expanses of nature.

Vacation land and sky: they nourish the seed deeply planted in us as children, the seed that first showed us the world as a shining, awesome place. The concerns of adulthood often dry out that seed, but it always remains within us, waiting for moisture.

———

I have to check in, frequently, with loneliness — *my* loneliness — the way others call their answering service. I have to touch base with it to reestablish a familiar continuity with my essential self. I have to verify that certain needs that have been part of me all my life — that I do not understand and probably never will — are still intact: half-hidden, inscrutable, but as important to me as breath and blood.

This afternoon is the present.

But the afternoons of my past were this same present too. The past is not past.

Somehow today and a day millions of years ago are the same continuous moment.

Eternity is always now.

People live out their lives without being devastated by the fact that they live and die in relative obscurity on a pinprick of a globe in a humanly unfathomable universe among possibly untold other universes. They make a kind of peace with their lot by accepting astounding religious explanations of the world and their momentary place in it.

Trees: they have the fluidity of the seas, the serene majesty of the skies, the unspoken depths of unconscious thought. They have the gracefulness of dancers in a group. They are classic and romantic. They seem to offer more than we know how to receive.

Others seem comfortable compartmentalizing the universe into Mother Earth (responsible for flowers and babies), God the Father (dealing in sin, punishments, salvation), and Some Other Force (classified as evil or the devil or natural disaster).

I want to ask those who believe that God created the heavens and the earth if God, when they think of Him, is separate from what they think of as nature? Is the God of the Old Testament who sent plagues upon Egypt and destroyed Sodom and Gomorrah no longer involved in natural events? Does He, or does He not, involve Himself in post-Bible times in plagues, hurricanes, earthquakes?

———

Several years ago 1,400 religious pilgrims died at Mecca after the air-conditioning in a tunnel failed. They were stampeded to death in the 112 degree heat, and King Fahd of Saudi Arabia said it was God's will. An air-conditioning unit fails and people who are crowded into a narrow, suffocating tunnel panic, trample each other, and die: God's will.

When a rock slide in Peru crushes 2,000 villagers, or a flood drowns 5,000 people in Bangladesh, or an earthquake kills 30,000 Iranians, religious leaders often make King Fahd's familiar pronouncement. God's will.

Chance, providence, fate, destiny, accident, predestination, God's will: I have never known what to make of such terms.

As we live here in a little corner of our galaxy, humans have settled on some fiercely held concepts they cannot

always prove but for which they will kill and die: sin and salvation, evil and damnation, God's will and God's judgments.
A sparrow falls, a lily toils, a baby burns up in a tenement fire, Hiroshima vaporizes in a mushroom cloud, Jews die by the millions in the Holocaust, blossoms form on the peach trees in the spring, the sun keeps coming up in the east.

What to think about such things?

I started out in my teens determined to figure it all out—God and religion and the meaning of life—and gave it, I think, a very good shot. I tried. I read and considered, and I mulled it over and read some more. I spent fifty years of my life in a dogged search for truth.

I finally quit. I don't believe any human has ever had a clue about the origin of life or the meaning of life. I also believe that religious dogmatism, religious intransigence, religious conflict have been as great a stumbling block to human peace and sanity as any other force.

We really don't know. We live in absolute ignorance of how it is with life, with the universe.

I don't believe in sin. I don't believe in an afterlife. But it doesn't matter at all what I believe or what anyone believes. It only matters what is.

———

It was the time of another day's lush ending as I walked along quiet streets in east El Paso: the pastel sky, the well-tended lawns, the elegant poplars, the masses of red-and-white oleanders. The cloud shadows stretched in front of a low white sun, and doves raced overhead as if delivering some final edition of the earth's news before sundown.

It was the time of desert day nearing desert night; it was neighbor women—paused, their babies lying safe within their strollers—standing and talking on the sidewalk beside neat hedges and walkways and garages; it was cats curled into the proper spaces of themselves beneath Mexican elder trees.

It was the end of the day with death nowhere in sight— as if death could not exist amid so much suburban tranquility. It was imperturbable daily life winding smoothly down, life as a continuous placid ocean with humans comfortably, innocently afloat.

———

As the years pass and I get older than I ever wanted to be, I have the urge to call up those from whom I have drifted away or who have drifted away from me. I want to say: We're foolish, you know, to have given up on each other so easily, so carelessly, to have pulled away so defensively, to have become stiff-necked, self-protective, unforgiving— whatever we are—and to have failed to continue to be the us we once were. We drifted apart, and the years became decades, yet out of stubbornness and an exaggerated sense of pride we will never again hear the other's voice as the final doors close quietly around us.

——

It was out of the space reserved for me that I was able to write at all. It was this private place that I did not want to give up—that I knew, instinctively, was essential. Yet it was precisely this space that early on, in my twenties, the females in my life sensed I kept from them: the private part of me that prevented me from being completely theirs. It was this space, they felt, that denied them the sense of security they needed from me—and that I wanted to keep separate for my own survival.

I was willing to give up this space only when the threat of loss—the complete loss of the other—was greater than my need for my individuality, my personal fulfillment, my identity, which I could have only through the words I could write in my own space.

——

After a long absence from writing I come back to the typewriter, and I cannot make the words move. They have become heavy weights. I resist them—or, fancifully, they resist me. I am uncomfortable trying to use them.

The very words that enabled me to function during much of my adult life are like strangers. They offer no salvation and certainly no pleasure.

Occasionally I look at pages of old notes and I have a physical revulsion as I reread them—not because of their content but simply out of a deep distancing, an estrangement. I have become a lapsed believer in the act of writing.

I am like a lover who once, over and over, carefully touched the features of a loved one with his fingertips—absorbed in his attention, his dedication—and now cannot find any interest in tracing the cold marble of his love's remains.

PART FOUR

Central Texas

The Spell

On summer days when I was a boy I sat on the ground beneath the clothesline and played "ranch" with rocks and sticks and acorns. The clothesline stretched across the bare slope of our backyard—from a post at the corner of the yard to the old wooden garage—and from mid-morning to hot summer noontime I played in and out of the shadows of the cup towels and my father's khaki shirts. I would dig and scoop and tear down corrals and fences of my little pretend ranch, and then I would stop and sit, look around and just sort of be there in the full blaze of the hill country heat and familiarity of our back-yard. I listened to the sparrows in the surrounding oaks. I looked at the red ants crawling in the sun toward their pebbly, whitened holes. I sat for long stretches of child-hood time—quiet, watching, absorbed in being next to the ground.

Years later, as I remembered those backyard moments—the way the hard-packed, rocky earth gleamed with a bright, almost radiant intensity just inches from my face—it seemed that the ground was almost capable of speech. It seemed that I—that boy bent over in his midday play—could have heard the earth talk if I had only known how to listen.

Since childhood I have been waiting, in some way, for just such a moment to occur: to be walking along and have the sides of buildings or cedar posts or the earth itself begin to speak. I have been ready for inanimate objects to break the spell that has held them silent—for trees to start talking in their quiet tree voices, telling me things I already knew somehow but could never put into words.

The Unexpected Other

We are all captives of certain childhood experiences that help determine the direction of our lives. I remember when I was five or six years old and my mother took me on walks at the edge of town. We went out on a narrow road past cedars and oaks and up an incline toward the top of a hill that overlooked the town. We would stop and turn around and look back across the valley. Mother would point to where our house was hidden among the trees, and then she showed me the school buildings and the Methodist church and, farther on, the railroad cars lined up beside my father's feed store.

But it is not that panoramic view from the hill that I kept remembering over the years. It is nothing remarkable, really—just a part of the roadside and the smooth, sunlit caliche embankment that ran along next to it.

Just that: the sun gleaming on a stretch of white dirt.

I have no idea why that place and that moment have stuck with me for nearly seventy years—what that mild glare of late-afternoon sun meant to me and why I have kept the memory of it alive so clearly.

Was it my first glimpse of the Unexpected Other in life—the blank face of mystery, of the humanly unknowable briefly glimpsed among the hillside Spanish oaks and sycamores?

In some curious way did I accept, without understanding it, a fundamental challenge? Is that what I was trying to do all my adult life: attempting to fill in that empty space, that stretch of smooth white dirt by putting onto blank paper word after word?

Neighbors

Today people uproot and resettle and close the front door of their most recent house and don't think very much or care very much about who the neighbors are if they keep the stereo down and don't have a barking dog at night. Then a job opens up in another part of the country or military orders come through saying Germany or North Carolina, and here comes the moving van again and a realtor's sign reappears in the front yard and it will be as if those people, whoever they might have been, were never there. They left no trace.

It was not that way when I was growing up in the 1930s. *Neighbors* was a word rich in connotations and specifics. It meant the Laughlins in the next block and Miss Mitchell next door and the Selfs on the corner and the Leifestes catty-corner from us and the Coldwell boys who smoked Bull Durham and went barefoot in the wintertime and Old Man Taylor who lived down below the hill and during the summer lay on a cot beneath the trees in his undershirt and cursed whichever of his kids or grandkids was handy. They were people who had been in the neighborhood all my life. Nobody moved much in those days. In Kerrville neighbors were as fixed as the trees and hills, the times of day, and I was who I was partly because of them.

We kept a cow in our back lot and sold extra milk to the neighbors. When I was eight or nine, one of my weekly chores was to deliver two quarts of milk to Miss Bertie Barrett, who lived in a small corner house down the street.

With a bottle of milk in each hand I went through her backyard and up the steps to her screened-in back porch. She would open the door and take the bottles: a slight, quick moving, always smiling, always cheerful gray-haired woman.

Even after we sold the cow and stopped delivering milk I passed Miss Bertie's corner house as I walked the two blocks back and forth to school. Sometimes she would be there on her front porch, sitting in the swing, and she would smile and wave at me. Or she would be bent over, working in her flower bed beneath the living room window.

There were never any complaints, never any frowns from Miss Bertie. She had what I later learned was called a southern attitude — a constant courtesy, a gracious, self-deprecatory manner. Whenever she talked to my mother or to me she would lean a bit to one side, her hand to her mouth, and speak in a low-pitched, confidential, almost conspiratorial way, and then finish with a light little laugh, as if to minimize everything she had just said.

I didn't know how long her niece, Margie, lived with her. She was a few years older than I was — pretty, soft-fleshed, very serious and studious. After high school she went off to college and became a biochemist.

But Miss Bertie kept on being Miss Bertie. She sat on her porch swing in the late afternoon, reading or looking across the street at the children playing on the elementary school grounds. She got smaller and more white-haired, but she smiled at me as I walked by and she gave her little wave.

Sammy Laughlin, my best friend when I was in elementary school, had big canine teeth and black hair that he kept shiny with Brilliantine and that always fell down across his forehead. He was solidly built, and if he had been meaner he would have been a bully at school and in the neighborhood. But mainly he just had a daredevil streak and liked to mess up things. He would come over, and sometimes we played Monopoly on the front porch. But usually we roamed around the back lots. He chased the chickens off their nests and they came squawking out of the henhouse — Sammy in the middle of them, hair down in his eyes, grinning at me through the cloud of dust and feathers.

Or he would take a stick and tease the Coldwells' dog through the wire fence until the dog nearly went crazy. If he found a wasp nest under the eaves of the garage, he would spend half the morning throwing rocks at it, trying to knock it down. He liked to catch horned toads sitting by the red ant bed next to the garden, hold them close to his face, and see if they would really spit blood out of their eyes, as everybody said they did.

We would go to his house and get cold water from the old vinegar bottle they kept in the ice box. The Laughlins' kitchen always smelled like cooked cabbage and sour laundry. Mrs. Laughlin would come inside from hanging clothes on the line, and she would ask if we wanted something else to drink. We would sit at the oilcloth-covered table for a while, drinking Kool-Aid out of Mason jars.

Mr. Laughlin was out of work, and he would sit there in the kitchen at midday, unshaven and in his undershirt and old slippers. Smoke from his cigarette curled above his head while the cabbage bubbled and steamed on the stove. He sat with his long legs crossed, ignoring Mrs. Laughlin and Sammy and me. He just smoked and dangled one of his slippers and stared out the screen doorway into the chinaberry shade of the backyard.

Home Town, 1943

Kerrville was my town the way my family was my family. I belonged to it, in it, the way the summer sun belonged in the central Texas sky, the way my father belonged to the dim, dusty feed store, the way my mother belonged to the back sleeping porch in the midafternoon, sitting beside the ironing board on the old roll-up barber's stool and ironing shirts.

It was my town, and at twelve I was old enough to walk by myself if I went to the show, or to buy comic books, or to follow the railroad tracks all the way to the feed store when, like this afternoon, I had left the house and was going to help out Daddy from three o'clock until closing time. The oaks in the neighbors' yards, the radios playing through their window screens—they were as familiar to me as the rattle of Daddy's truck turning into the back lot in the late afternoon.

Head down, I watched my shoes and the cuffs of my khaki pants as they went along the trail through the vacant lot by the school—through the peppergrass, the weeds—on the way to town. ("To town"—that's how everybody said it, not "downtown" or "the center of town." When a neighbor said "I'm going to walk to town," that meant he was going where Earl Garrett Street and Water Street met, the main blocks that had the post office and J.C. Penney's and the Arcadia Theatre and Pampell's Drug Store and Heckler's Men's Store and the Charles Schreiner Bank.)

I walked diagonally across the vacant lot, stopped in at

the Red and White grocery store on the corner and bought a Popsicle and then went along the cracked sidewalk past the Heard house. At three o'clock it was still too hot for Mr. Heard to be outside, but I knew that in a little while he would be sitting in his chair on the front lawn reading the paper. Mr. Heard, who was retired, always looked up when a car passed by and waved at anyone he recognized and then went back to his paper. Mrs. Heard gave piano lessons, and sometimes in the late afternoon I could see the outline of her through the window and hear somebody practicing.

I passed the chiropractor's small white frame house that was set back from the street. My mother had made me go there three or four times the year before; she thought the treatments — adjustments, they were called — would help my asthma. There was a little front waiting room that had a linoleum floor. Whenever I came there and waited I would read *Collier's* magazines and sit in a metal folding chair like the ones in the basement activity room at school, and finally Red would come out of a back room and then Rose came too. I suppose Rose was his wife. She stood by a potted plant and smiled. Red always had his shirt off and wore old crepe-soled shoes and white pants. His chest was sunburned from sunbathing or maybe a sun lamp and had a lot of curling, reddish hair on it. Rose was dark — like what I thought a gypsy looked like — and she wore flowery, kind of long dresses instead of a uniform. Red had talked to my mother about how important it was to "follow nature's way," which I guess meant not to take a lot of medicines and to keep coming to him. I couldn't tell if the adjustments ever helped my asthma any.

I cut across the lawn of the Presbyterian church, and I wondered again what it was that the Presbyterians did there that was different from other churches. Their scout troop was #155—I knew that much—but I don't think I ever knew anybody who was Presbyterian. The concrete steps that went up the main entrance were big wide ones, and they looked just as hard for old ladies to climb on Sunday mornings as ours did at the Methodist church.

In the middle of the next block, at Unnasche Cleaners, I saw old Mr. Unnasche bent over at his worktable, making alterations. I could feel the heavy heat of the shop coming through the front doorway, and I could hear the blast of steam swishing through a hole in the building into the outside weeds. Mrs. Unnasche looked up from her sewing machine and smiled at me through the sidewalk window as I walked around the corner of their shop toward the railroad tracks.

I liked the long, open sweep going beside the tracks and the smell of the hot creosote on the railroad ties. A truck from Grona's Lumber Yard drove past me, and the white caliche dust rose from the unpaved street and hung in the air for a long while before settling down on the hackberry trees beside the tracks. The sun was bearing down now, and in the hackberries the locusts were singing hard. The sound of them rose up, like a siren almost, then each time flattened to a long locust hum. It was a good sound, like the very sound a hot summer afternoon should make.

In the distance I could see the wide dock and the big, open doors of the wool and mohair building, and then I could see right on through the doors where the heavy wool sacks were piled up out of sight. Just beyond the mohair building I could make out the figure of my father as he walked back and forth across a plank set up between the feed store and a railroad car full of blocks of sulfur salt.

Blocks of salt shipped in today, I thought. Okay, they're about right for me to lift. I can stack four or five of them at a time on the dolly. That's always kind of fun.

And I hurried on in the heat.

Home, at Sundown

One of the chores I did when I was growing up was feeding the chickens. Each afternoon at five-thirty or six I opened the door of the old garage and got the coffee can and dipped it down into the sack of chicken feed inside the door. I turned and began to scatter the grain to the White Leghorns that came running from the patch of Sudan grass below the garden and into the rocky, open space by the garage. I stood there, tossing out handfuls to the chickens and to the small Mexican doves that always slipped down from the trees and walked about like little bobbing mechanical toys. The sun was going down beyond the oak trees just west of our house; the pigeons were strutting about in the cages beside the cow shed; yells were coming from the softball game in the park a block away.

I never thought I was doing anything special on those fall afternoons. Tossing out grain was as normal as breathing. I was thirteen, it was the end of the day, I was at home—the only home I had ever lived in, had ever known—and it was almost time for my father to close up his feed store and come rattling in his pickup truck down the rocky street beside our house and turn in at the sagging, wooden gate and come to a stop beneath the backyard clothesline. He would be there, his profile in the cab, his old work hat on, with traces of laying mash across the brim, and he would raise his arm to me in his brief end-of-the-day salute. I would finish shaking out the last of the grain from the coffee can and run over to him as he lifted out the grocery sack of coffee and bread and fried pies.

That was all it was, just a sundown moment with chickens and doves and pigeons and the sun low in the trees and my father coming in from work. It would be years before I understood that such a moment was what home was all about when I was growing up: a place of unspectacular and satisfying contentments. I never felt I needed more, or something different, because what I had, every day—so simple, so ordinary—was always enough.

Big Band Days

Some of the young people today stick studs in their tongues, spike their hair, put on their black clothes and heavy boots, and stride rather fiercely forth, almost challenging the world to *just say something about how I look, I dare you.* They are marking their territory, asserting—they hope—their uniqueness. In the late 1940s I did not feel a need to do that kind of rebellious stuff, but by discovering Stan Kenton I knew I was on a special path. At least I felt I was part of something hugely removed from the ordinary.

Kenton. Just his name, that single word, summed it up: the excitement of New Music, New Sounds. His arrangements, his personnel were red meat placed before me on a table that had previously been set with bowls of cold oatmeal. "Intermission Riff," "Collaboration," "Artistry in Bolero," "Artistry in Rhythm," "The Peanut Vendor," "Concerto to End All Concertos"—I played them until I could anticipate every note, cue every solo. I loved his trumpets—the solid massed intensity of them—flashing, screaming, soaring like sudden bursts of silver; his trombones, moaning, full-throated, majestic. Kenton himself rippling away stylishly on piano; the rasping, gruff eloquence of Vido Musso on tenor sax; Eddie Safranski, like a light-fingered thief slipping through the music with his bass; and from time to time, bright and shiny, the voice of June Christy who, as she told us, was "Just A-Sittin' and A-Rockin.'"

I learned Kenton the way other guys were learning Cars.

But what I was actually learning about was the whole Big Band era: the songs, the singers, the sidemen, the arrangements, the instrumentalists. At the downtown Kerrville record store, I bought, whenever I could get together enough money, the Decca and Capitol and Columbia 78s of Benny Goodman, Woody Herman, Harry James, Artie Shaw, and Les Brown.

And the Duke.

To a kid growing up in Kerrville—where at summer noon the Light Crust Doughboys were on the neighborhood radios and at night the drive-in customers fed their nickels into the jukebox for Ernest Tubb—Duke Ellington was like nothing I had ever heard. His creations were so new to my small-town ears that they seemed like exotic calls from a rain forest. The singers sounded like instruments; the instruments sounded like voices.

I played them in a kind of trance: "Caravan," "Solitude," "Mood Indigo," "Sophisticated Lady." I listened to the strange, haunting harmonies, the deft distortions of sound, the notes that drifted dreamily and then faded. It was like watching wavy images underwater or sinuous dancers in masks swaying, leaning, collapsing, rising, throwing arms here and there.

On "East St. Louis Toodle-oo" the trumpeter, Cootie Williams, growled his way through a chorus, then ended with some harsh, slashing *wha-acks*, as if from metallic whips. On "Creole Love Call" the singer, Kay Davis, gave out not a song but a kind of sustained, mournful, effortless, wordless cry. On "Black and Tan Fantasy" Barney Bigard's clarinet kept rising like a sleek bird soaring higher and higher until it burst and showered sound like a Roman candle.

I probably had not seen a Picasso drawing while I was in high school, but if I had come across one I surely would have looked long at it and thought, Man, that's what Duke Ellington is all about.

Then there were the first ascending notes of "I'm Getting Sentimental Over You." They were enough, each time, to make the goose bumps come — not just because they were the signal that Tommy Dorsey's radio broadcast was about to start but because that limpid tone of his represented the pure sound that I — aspiring high school trombone player that I was — kept yearning for. Dorsey made his horn sing as no other trombonist did. He was no great shakes as a jazzman — actually rather flatfooted and uninspired — but on "Song of India" and "Marie" he just plain shimmered. When it was sign-off time at the end of his program and he began to repeat his "Sentimental" theme song, I always ached a little as I sat hunched over next to the radio, hearing those lovely notes disappear and leave a sadness in their place.

At the Pavilion

I was seventeen in the spring of my senior year, and my date and I were seated with other couples at a small outdoor dance pavilion on the river road from Kerrville to Hunt. A string of yellow lights glowed above the cement square of the dance floor.

I remember the nearby oaks and cedars, the massed presence of them that led up a hill behind us, and now and then I could hear from across the road the sound of cars moving along the low-water bridge that went over the Guadalupe.

It was after eleven o'clock on a Friday night, and most of the people who had been eating inside the café had gone. It was just the six of us left at our table.

We would feed nickels into the jukebox and dance to "Laura" and "Adios" and "Till the End of Time." Anne, my date, was pretty with sort of crinkly, short brown hair—we had been going together since our junior year—and her breasts fit snugly against my chest as we danced.

When we left we drove out of the gravel parking lot in a half-circle before reaching the road to town. I remember glancing back at the lights of the pavilion—and it has been those lights that have stayed with me for over fifty years. Their dim glow has kept alive the spring night and the jukebox songs and the undercurrent of romance, the smell of the river among the trees—undying yellow gleams marking the end of youth.

Grona's Crossing

At Grona's Crossing on the Llano River the river is wide and shallow and spacious, and humped granite mounds lie scattered along the sandbars like little white and rose igloos left by ice-age Eskimos.

One afternoon I stood on the bank among the sunflowers and willows, fishing in one of the pools—waiting for a perch to leave its hiding place in the shadow of a ledge. The sun at midday was strong, seeming to lift the whiteness out of the nearby rocky shelf and fuse it to the bright summer air.

Across the river slender sycamores lined the bank, making a clean fresh rim for the Llano as it came curving out of the west. The bank itself was flat and neat with white, washed gravel on its shore.

Behind me a high bluff lifted sharply against the sky. When I grew tired of fishing, I climbed to the top of the bluff and stood among the lichen-spotted flint rocks and stunted cedars. I could see the road to Cedar Springs as it wound into mesquite-and-red-dirt country, into yuccas and agaritas. No river lushness up there, and no river-bottom farmland, but it was not inhospitable or foreboding, not High Lonesome.

Nothing moved. I stood there, and I did not move either. It was as if that was what I must do to earn the right to listen to the quiet, the land; to become aware of the shadow presence of the long-ago Comanches still lingering in the air of the low, blue surrounding hills.

Shade

Sun and shade. They are equal glories, and I have thrived mightily on both of them.

When I was in college, I bought a pair of clip-on sunglasses because, in my innocence, I thought that was what I was supposed to do: deny the sun, take the teeth out of its glare, see the world through a softening lens. Luckily I misplaced the glasses and never bought another pair; I went on experiencing hot Texas days in their full, burning splendor.

I like the sun. I need it. I flourish in its illuminating power and enjoy landscapes made vivid and distinct within its burning light. I walk about, staring contentedly at fields, mountains, and roadsides spread out beneath the sun's godly blaze.

But there are equally satisfying pleasures made possible by shade. Shade. The word is rich with, well, shadings. It does not, to me, imply darkness or somberness—carries no hint of Dante's shades, of melancholy ghosts or spirits. It suggests places of refuge or rest, of contemplation. It carries a positive air: to be "in the shade" is poetry, not desperation.

I have good memories of shade. When I was growing up, I spent whole summer afternoons on the front porch of my grandparents' ranch, sitting in the green, curved-back chair and looking out at the yard, the flower beds, the front clearing, the sheep lying in shadowed clumps beneath the trees. I think it was there, on those long and spacious afternoons, that I became a serious spectator of life-as-a-personal-drama. As I sat on the porch with my feet up, I gazed outward, I looked at the wasps and plum trees and the sky, and I began reaching for a pencil to record it all.

Other times, on Sundays, my family and I would drive out on hill country back roads and find a spot along a creek to spread old quilts beneath the sycamores. And while my father fished and my mother read, I sat next to the ice chest and smelled the fried chicken and homemade cookies in the picnic basket and watched the sunlight on the water and heard the creek running across the rocks. It was the best kind of Sunday there beneath the trees.

All across central Texas there are creeks and rivers and trees—and elegant areas of shade. In my college years I worked as a summer camp counselor, and during lazy mid-afternoons in our cabin, while the eight-year-olds drifted into their naps, I would look out the screened window toward the cypresses bordering the Guadalupe River below the hill. The luring line of greenery told of free swim soon to come at four o'clock and—before supper—of long, leisurely canoe rides within the deep cypress canopy.

Texas has a bright sky, and most people retreat from its uncompromising intensity. City people tint their car windows; rural men clamp down their wide-brimmed hats closer to their eyes. But from the pecan tree bottoms of the Nueces River to the mesquite flats of the Edwards Plateau, trees provide—for those who seek it out—an oasis, a sanctuary.

Nobody Whistles Anymore

When I was growing up it seemed as if everybody whistled at one time or another. It was like breathing or smiling or saying hello. Or feeding the dog, watering the lawn, reading the newspaper in the front room. Whistling was just a normal thing for people to do. Kids whistled as they rode their bikes across a vacant lot. Garage mechanics whistled walking around the raised hood of a car they were working on. My grandmother whistled—not truly, not with a brisk shrillness, but breathily, softly, almost tunelessly, just to herself, as she moved about her ranch kitchen at ten o'clock in the morning getting the meal ready for dinnertime. High school boys whistled in self-assured confidence as they walked toward the front door of their date's house on Saturday night.

Postmen seemed to be the most spirited, most memorable whistlers in my home town. Mr. Michon was a short, wiry, red-faced man who seemed to thrive on carrying his mail pouch block after block—walking onto porches and paying no attention to the dogs behind screen doors or in the side yards, then walking back out into the brief shade of oaks and chinaberries—and all the while whistling to the morning, the sunshine, the town. He was regular as clockwork in every neighborhood, and his whistle always preceded him by half a block.

But something happened after I grew up. Whistling just seemed to die away. Maybe people became weighted down by serious concerns and felt they had no time to waste on trivial matters—but I don't believe that was really the reason. (Americans continued to whistle during the Depression, during World War II . . .) As best I can figure, whistling began to disappear sometime in the 1960s— about the time that poetry began to shrivel up and die in public school classrooms; when Vietnam became our national preoccupation; when disaffected youth in blue jeans discovered drugs and racism and the various imperfections of their elders; when Broadway show tunes and other romantic, melodic songs gave way to the grim expressions of social protest.

A person whistles when his psyche is in equilibrium, when there is a simplicity in his heart and a buoyancy in his soul. A person whistling in his car is like a bird tootling in a tree. Has the complexity of modern life rendered us incapable of joy in the morning and a sense of freedom in the afternoon? Is the inability to whistle an indictment of our present national character or just a negligible absence of something not very important anyway?

Maybe the topic is one for the scholars. Maybe we will have to wait for a Harvard sociologist—or any properly serious-minded fellow—to publish his dissertation, "Whistling: Its Origins and Ramifications as Reflected in the Psychoanalytically Oriented Studies of Multicultural Populations." I might read such a weighty treatise but— like my grandmother—I'll be whistling softly under my breath.

Peas

After my divorce I moved from El Paso to San Antonio and began living, again, the solitary life.

One afternoon after I had finished teaching I stopped by H-E-B and stood in a brightly lit aisle beside a row of canned peas. I regarded the cans with distaste—as if they were filled with pain, not peas. I was going to select one of them even though the peas would not be poured into a family pan on a family stove in a family kitchen. I would be opening the can for myself in a small apartment, listening to the sound of a television news analyst instead of the voices of my children. I did not want the peas any more than I wanted the bag of Fritos that I was carrying, or the loaf of bread. I did not want any of the shiny cans of vegetables stacked neatly in front of me, or any of the fruits from the produce bins, or any of the packaged meats. I had no interest in buying food that would be prepared and eaten alone.

Standing in the aisle—a grim, graying ghost of a shopper—I recalled other years, other food stores at the end of the day in El Paso when I was still married. I remembered entering the casual after-work community of neighborhood shoppers at the Big 8 near my home, disentangling a cart from the other carts near the entrance, and pushing it slowly past the bakery counter into the heart of the store. As I took a can of pineapple from the shelf, the intercom called for a checker to come to the front. I turned toward the canned juices and saw the checker—the teenaged son of our next-door neighbor—loping past, clomping along the floor in his desert boots, waving at me and smiling as he wiped his wet hands against his apron.

That's the way shopping ought to be, I thought—the way it was for eighteen years. Personalized, with families and neighbors in mind.

I selected a can of Del Monte Early June Peas and started down the aisle toward the checkout lanes. I stood dutifully in line, waiting my turn. I paid for my small sack of groceries, nodded when the checkout girl thanked me and gave me my receipt. I spoke to no one as I left the store.

I got into my car and drove to my apartment. I shifted the sack to my other hand, put the key in the door, opened it, and went inside. I threw the peas into the trash.

Byron and I

We had fished the jetties at Port Aransas, looked across Llano country from Enchanted Rock, drifted down the Frio River beneath the cypresses at Garner Park, and now—well, we were just going out from Kerrville to the west pasture of the family ranch place to camp for a while. My son, Byron, and I and a dog.

We loaded the Chevy hatchback with boxes and quilts and the compact, two-man nylon tent from K-Mart that almost fit in your pocket, and we eased out into the four o'clock June heat. Byron's solemn-eyed dog, Duchess, was curled on the front seat by the air conditioner. Byron lay in back among the boxes. He was reading a comic, his legs angled upward above the Styrofoam cooler. I gazed at the passing fields, then looked once more into the rearview mirror at Byron's toes: they were pieces of sculpture, those white, narrow feet and ankles, those pleasantly curved bones, that shining flesh. I drove on, enjoying the country-side, but I kept glancing at the symmetry of my son's feet freed from shoes and upraised in the air. There was nothing exotic about them; they were just ordinary, human boy-bones suddenly delicate, suddenly strange, like white undersea flowers that had joined together in the hatchback light.

We turned off the Mountain Home highway and drove upward toward the ranchland plateau. Some of the pastures were unfenced, and sheep lay in the road in the shade of the trees. I drove slowly around them, then saw it again: the Oehler home. It was a ranch house I had admired—coveted—for thirty years, an unpretentious rock house set in a clump of oaks. There was a garden in back, a neat wire fence, a rock garage, a front porch with an arched entrance. Sitting there, in just the right blend of shadow and sun, just off the road enough, with just the right amount of yard, it had always represented to me the beauty one strove for, the peace one wanted, the home in the country at the end of the day.

At the gate to our property Byron got out, started undoing the chains around the post. As he stood there, trying to make the worn key fit the lock, I found it a pleasure to look at him: my son, twelve, almost thirteen, in his worn blue tank top, blue shorts, Nike tennis shoes without socks. I liked seeing him do that—open the gate finally and swing it forward, then stand beside it in the rising bit of dust, waiting for me to drive on through. My son the apprentice guitar player, the seventh-grade drummer, the lover of loud Rush rock songs; my son, his Prince Valiant–style blond hair shining in the sun, his mother's features nicely chromosomed in his face.

The road to the hunting cabin was rocky, almost impassable; we eased along it for half a mile and stopped at the ridge that overlooked the small valley to the south. It was a classic amphitheater of grassland, with tree-lined knolls on both sides. We got out and stood in the country stillness. A buzzard was circling high overhead. A mockingbird was holding a private carnival in the top of a post oak. Thistles—hundreds of them below the ridge—wobbled their purple heads like Martian shock troops that had descended onto the ranchland in the heat. They were tall, slender and spiny, but their heads—all slightly turned, all at angles—were demure, beautifully round, as if they were all wearing brilliant Martian afros.

We selected a level spot to set up the tent, facing it south to catch the breeze. Byron assembled it in a professional manner—tightening a rope here, realigning another there—and soon it became a bright orange envelope staked neatly to the earth. He called Duchess, and they raced down into the valley. Beer in hand, I watched them a long while, the way you look at a painting.

They returned, and Byron and I began to horse around with Country Talk. "Hey, boy," I said, "you better find me some cedar bark if we gonna have any vittles tonight." Byron said, "Shore, Paw," and raced Duchess across the rocks and needle grass to a big cedar tree. He returned with enough long strips to start the campfire. Then he got his BB gun and roamed around shooting at gourds, dragonflies, scorpions under rocks. He stopped a moment and said in a mock gunfighter's drawl, "Wal, cow patty, we meet again," and fired four quick ones into the soggy pile.

"Reckon we better clear the land, Paw?" Byron called out. He got a gray, weather-smooth limb from a brush pile and began chopping down the tall mullein plants along the ridge with loud kung fu *haaaaaas*. He stopped and stared at a formidable-looking plant in front of him.

"He just called you a bad name, Paw."

"A bad name!" I said in my own Yosemite Sam voice. "Well, git him, Son!"

Byron swung his stick viciously, toppling the bad-mouthing plant.

By seven o'clock the breeze was sweeping the ridge. I sat on a canvas campstool in the shade of the car, reading. Byron returned from another round of exploration with Duchess. He drank a root beer from the cooler; his fuel-injected belches rocked the air.

Time passed and the ridge was quiet. A plane droned by. Then, from inside the hatchback: "Dad, what does girth mean?" A bit later: "What does bauble mean?" Welcome questions to me. They meant that Byron had made himself a place among the quilts and was reading a library book. *The Black Cauldron* was a sword-clasher full of huntsmen and enchantresses and characters with alphabet-stew names like Orgoch, Lluagor, and Fflewwdur, but I was pleased that he had picked it up—I had tossed it into the car next to his BB gun in order to tempt him—and that he cared to ask about words. This had been a historic summer: he had cut back on watching television and discovered reading. He had made his way through all seven books in *The Chronicles of Narnia* by C. S. Lewis. He liked the Olden Days.

Shadows stretched; mourning doves began to call. We found a suitable place for a fire in the rocky crack that ran down the ridge to the valley floor. It had a good draft, no grass around it to catch fire. We carried big rocks, shaped a fireplace, arranged other rocks around it to make, roughly, a surrounding table. We built our fire.

I brought the hamburger meat and the pan from the car and Byron started cooking. He put a strip of bacon on top of each mound of meat. I sat nearby on a rock stool I had fashioned, savoring the smoke smell, the hamburger smell.

I went up to the car, got another beer, looked about. Streams of eight o'clock light touched, washed, surrounded the tree trunks as they stood in the pasture. It was an intimate scene—as if the trees had finally taken off their clothes at sundown and were chastely bathing up to their knees in a sea of reddish, primordial light flowing in from the west.

We ate our hamburgers and small cherry tomatoes and Fig Newtons. We put on more wood to keep the fire going. At nine o'clock the first pale star appeared above the ridge. Katydids began to pulse in the trees. We listened: sure enough, an owl was in the trees to the east of us. We listened again: another owl answered, farther away.

I slapped at mosquitoes and Byron poked at the fire.

"Tell me again about the ranch," he said, "when you came out as a boy." It was dark now. "What did you like best?"

He was talking about the ranch house when my grandparents lived there—when it was still a working ranch, a lifestyle, when there were sheep and goats and horses and mules and hired hands and gardens and grain fields and homemade ice cream and large family gatherings. He had missed out on all of that. My grandfather had already died when Byron was born; he barely remembered my grandmother as a shrunken old woman in a Kerrville nursing home who gave him Juicy Fruit gum and candy orange slices. He had looked at all the family albums, heard anecdotes about relatives he had never seen, stayed in the ranch house before it was sold. He had sat in the chairs that Gram and Grandpa sat in, had eaten at their dining table. But it was as though the ranch was a half-century-long parade he had just barely missed. It was as if there had been a family mirror that—if he could have looked into it—would have shown him the fullest possible picture of himself, but now it was broken.

So I talked a while about what the ranch was like when I was growing up. I told Bryon that those barren, rocky fields he and I once walked across, full of horehound, had been cornfields with stalks higher than Grandpa's head. I told him about Gram in her bonnet making lye soap in the wash pot on summer mornings—and the clean smell of the laundry flapping on the line. My best moment to remember? Well, I told him, maybe it was waking up in the featherbed in the west room, next to the garden, and hearing

Grandpa's boots clumping and scuffing on the sidewalk and then the gate creaking and slamming as he went into the back lot, and the sound of the windmill turning—slowly, easily, as if it would keep turning forever—and the lambs bleating up by the water tank, and Gram, with her hair in braids across her head and her apron on, coming across the linoleum floor in her worn canvas shoes, saying good morning and asking if I was ready for breakfast, and my saying yes, and stretching and turning beneath the covers, and then lying there, feeling perfect, smelling the biscuits through the bedroom door.

We let the fire die down after a while and looked up at the stars. It had been a long time since either of us had seen the sky at night in such an isolated country place. We stared, properly impressed, wanting to talk about what we saw but knowing there wasn't really much that could be said. The stars. They were there; my God, they were there. Byron knew about starlight, that what we thought we saw was really light that started out billions or trillions or quadrillions of years ago. We found the Big Dipper.

Duchess began barking far off in the valley, and we suddenly remembered her. Byron first called her; then he gave a whistle—an astonishingly shrill, penetrating two-fingered blast of sound I didn't know he had mastered—and we heard her coming. We decided she had found an armadillo.

"Want to go up to Harper?" I asked. It was nearly ten o'clock. We ought to crawl into our orange-colored cocoon for the night. But the question was suddenly there in my head.

"Sure," Byron said. "Maybe we can get a soda." My son the camper: not yet an ascetic, not yet willing to live on grubs and berries.

We drove back through the gate and up the farm-to-market road toward Harper. Windows down, we moved leisurely past the fields of corn, past the lanes and mailboxes—Goff, Klaehn, Wienecke, Kothmann. Byron had his arm out the window, letting it ride the air currents, ready to nab one of the grasshoppers that flared into the headlights. Duchess had her head in his lap.

It was a moment of pleasing darkness on a smooth back road, the wind so cool now it was almost cold. We were going up to Harper, population 383, just sort of because, I guessed. Because it was nearby, so why not; because Byron hadn't been there very often; because we were camped out in a pasture under a sky incredibly loaded with the rest of the universe and suddenly I had an impulse to touch base with the human community—any human community; because the drive up that particular road had always been pleasant.

The road curved, eased down into dips at dry branch crossings. Deer grazed along the roadside, their heads, eyes, bodies turned slightly toward our lights. Ranch houses sat unseen in an oak flat or on a cedar-cleared rise of ground. Sumacs grew like lush hedges in a park along the fencelines.

We drove slowly into town and down the single main street, looking at the dark stretch of houses and stores. There was the Modern Market where my uncle still bought groceries when he came in from his ranch. There was Harper High. There was the street to the cemetery where my grandparents and my father were buried. There was the pecan grove by the creek where we used to have family reunions when I was a child. We turned off the highway and looked into the quiet houses.

"What do you think it's like," I asked Byron, "living here every day in a small town like this—no movies, but a windmill in your backyard?" He didn't know what to think about it, about living there. Neither did I.

On the highway I stopped at the Longhorn Inn Cafe. Five or six people were seated at a table, talking casually in the weak overhead light. The ceiling fan was barely turning. A woman got up from the table; I bought two Sprites from her. Byron and I drove on back toward our pasture, drinking from the cold cans, satisfied with our little trip. Byron belched hugely into the night air.

The Ranch

In memory I can always return to the 1940s and my grand-parents' ranch. I can turn off the Harper highway at the cluster of rural mailboxes, go two miles through the neighbors' pastures of oaks and needle grass. I can bump over the last cattle guard and enter the ranch at the corner of the big oat field (the highest point in that part of the hill country, a surveyor once said). I can pause and look across the wide sweep of land toward the blue hills of the Guadalupe River valley to the south. Then I can drive the last 200 yards down the familiar oat field lane, and as I make the final curve I can see it again, as I saw it, child and grown-up, for over half a century: the front clearing, the yards, the ranch house with its green sloping roof, the top of the windmill through the post oaks, the peach orchard, the barn and corrals.

I can park beneath the big pecan tree next to the garage, get out of the car, pull the metal latch of the gate and hear it click behind me, continue up the cracked cement walk between the bordering flower beds. The Bermuda grass will be thick, in need of cutting. I can step onto the long concrete front porch—the walls still gray, the window frames trimmed in black—and after pulling open the screen door I can go into the small, cool living room with the grainy white vinyl couch against the east wall. (As a child I would look at those rough-textured walls—so different from our wallpapered walls at home—and touch their little dips of cream-colored plaster with pleasure.) I can take a long look at the smoke-darkened fireplace with the Seth Thomas clock on the mantel—the fireplace itself covered now in summertime by a portable panel—and at the two vinyl chairs in the fireplace corners. The room is not filled with light—just airy, inviting.

It is noon, and my grandfather is seated at the dinner table holding his glass of dark iced tea. My grandmother is seated too, nibbling at her corn bread. The cut-glass vinegar-and-oil bottle is still at its place in the center of the table, along with a bowl of garden okra, a saucer of sliced tomatoes, a plate of warmed-over pan-fried steak.

Invisible, I stand by the Cold Spot refrigerator and watch my grandfather as he sits in his accustomed place at the head of the table, his back to the front porch door. He has taken off his boots and is in his stocking feet. His white hair is plastered to the side—partly from the sweat of the old work Stetson he has been wearing all morning, partly from the splash of water and the brief rub of his hand when he washed up at the bathroom basin. My grandmother too sits in her accustomed place, in the first chair around from my grandfather's right side. She wears her hair up in a tight braid; she has on her print apron. They are talking, as always, about ranch matters, family matters—their voices without inflection or strong emotion, just steady and level, with long, unhurried pauses.

I can watch my grandfather idly drum his thick fingers as he looks through the lace window curtains toward the backyard post oak tree and the rock water tank and the noontime heat. I can watch my grandmother as she crumbles her corn bread into a saucer of milk and idly shoos away a fly.

I can watch, knowing that they will always be seated there at the table, that I can always come back.

On a Hillside

I was among oaks and cedars and grapevines on the south side of Kerrville. I was in a sunlit summer oven full of hot-earth smells, and I walked about in it gladly.

There were other lives around me—weed lives, wasp lives: hidden, buried, microscopic—and I stood among them like Gulliver in Lilliput. A universe was at work beneath my feet, and I could only guess at its dimensions. (I thought of termites I once read about, how they bang their heads on the floor in the dark in order to talk to one another.)

But the hillside and its intricate mysteries were doomed. Green high-voltage boxes were already in place; telephone poles stretched through a wide, cleared path. Sold signs were tacked here and there to trees. The developer's office sat beside a newly paved road.

I looked west across the fields, the Guadalupe River cypresses, the edge of town, and I saw other green hills, gashed now with new roads and expensive new homes.

Homeowners were coming to the hillsides. Within a year their sprawling ranch-style houses and satellite dishes would replace the post oaks and agarita bushes. Quail, deer, thistles, wild persimmon—all would be gone, as they were gone across the valley. Because the land had no rights.

I thought about this: people could own parts of the land and then sell those parts to other people who bought them. It was an old and accepted human practice. But the land itself had no say. Slavery had been abolished, but not earth-owning, earth-selling.

I walked across the hillside. Above me, clouds were performing their serene balancing acts in a fiercely blue sky. Locusts were everywhere in the trees, their shrill chorus rising and falling like the whine of miniature electric motors.

My watch said two-fifteen, but the minutes and hours were irrelevant here. It was earth time that I was on: leaf time, yucca time, caliche rock time.

A white grasshopper—who did not know or care about political parties or the Dallas Cowboys or wars in the Middle East—sat on a patch of needle grass and idly rubbed his body with a thin red leg. Behind him, in a patch of leaves, a small gray snake was carrying a centipede toward a crack in a lichened rock.

A breeze sprang up, blew against my sweat, cooled me. I stopped walking and stood in the shade as the fragile leaves of a Spanish oak began to shake. All about me was the hot-cedar incense, the strong, midday dirt and plant aromas.

I looked down and saw the pink plastic ribbon tied to a stake—I was standing on Lot 4—but it didn't matter too much. Not yet. Today, despite the developer's flags and the telephone poles, we were there peaceably together, this quiet hillside and I. I could still bathe in the immediacy of trees, ground, and sky.

Hackberry Afternoons

When I thought of hot summer days in east Austin, I remembered dust on weeds in junky side yards, discarded Popsicle wrappers on broken sidewalks, the throb of hillbilly jukebox music coming from a corner beer joint. I was in college then, roaming the streets—more concerned with trying to figure out life than with history and biology classes. It was as I walked those long hours in the neighborhoods of the poor—with heat bearing down through the constant, mindless whine of the locusts—that I began to think of them as "hackberry afternoons."

I had known such days when I was growing up: the sticky, midafternoon hours in June and July with laundry hanging on the clotheslines in our neighbors' yards, and radio programs—the fifteen-minute *Ma Perkins* and *Pepper Young's Family* soap operas of the 1930s—coming steadily from the open windows of nearby houses. I didn't pay any attention to the couple of hackberry trees in our yard—I was interested only in the big oaks where I built my tree houses—but I do remember how cars would drive by and raise the dust from the rocky street beside our house, and how the dust would drift and settle on the weeds and onto the rough leaves of the hackberries.

It was after I had graduated from college and started teaching around the state that hackberries finally took on their full symbolic role for me. They came to represent everything that was graceless and shabby and down-at-the-heels in the hot Texas summertime.

(I doubt that any homeowner ever planted a hackberry tree or encouraged its survival. Hackberries just appeared and then took hold in poor soil the way mesquites and cedar trees, if left alone, proliferated in pasturelands. Uninvited and unencouraged, they were like country squatters who came to town and stubbornly endured and thereby survived as the inelegant shade trees of low-rent areas, their rough-surfaced leaves becoming powdered with dust from unpaved streets that ran beside railroad tracks and warehouses and vacant lots.)

In my roamings around central Texas, I still gravitated toward these inelegant parts of town. I would be driving on a summer afternoon in San Saba, McGregor, Stephenville, or Llano and I would pull off the main drag and park my car and begin walking aimlessly down the hot side streets. Maybe I was still trying to lay to rest the ghosts of my growing-up days—the sights and sounds that were once part of my deepest reality and still had the power to haunt me, engage me, depress me. I studied the houses and once again saw that nothing had really changed. In one of the yards a baby sat in her barely pinned diaper, as if she had not moved in the last fifty years. She sat in smoothly shaded dirt beneath a tree—half-watched by an older sister who dangled her bare legs and gazed at the cars going by as she slowly revolved in a tire swing. A dog, half-asleep, lay with its nose on its paws beneath a sagging front porch.

I walked, squinting and sweating in the heat, along the cracked sidewalks past the overturned garbage cans. Television game shows instead of 1930s radio programs blared through living room windows. Dust still collected on the hackberry trees growing in the yellowed yards, and locusts still shrilled in their unending summer frenzy.

The Cabin Place

On summer mornings when I drove up to the family hunting cabin I always let a few of Talbot Garven's cows into the cabin lot to graze. They helped keep the grass down after the June rains, and I just liked to look at them from time to time as I worked about the place.

There wasn't much to do. Mr. Garven, who lived down the road to Harper, leased the pastures year-round for his cows, and he made the necessary, occasional repairs. None of my relatives and few family members ever made it out to the cabin. Everyone was scattered, and no one was particularly interested in leading the rural life anymore.

When my parents were alive—now that was a different story. They loved to come out to the Place, as they called it. While my father could still see to drive, they would take the back farm-to-market road from Kerrville and come out to the cabin on holidays and Sundays. It was a treat for them to get into the old green feed store pickup and bring barbecue or tuna fish sandwiches and check on their little herd of goats.

I remember watching my mother, in her seventies, leave the cabin in a light winter mist and walk up the low wooded hill toward the goat shed. I followed behind her. At first I thought she would make it to the top, but before long her arthritic knees began to throb and she had to stop and rest. She leaned against a sycamore and looked back toward the cabin, rubbing her knees and smiling down toward me. After a while she began to call in the high, singsong voice she had learned to use as a rancher's child growing up in the hill country: "Gooooatie, gooooatie, gooooatie." It was a clear, ringing falsetto call, and the goats, browsing along the side of the hill in a patch of shin oaks, lifted their heads, listened, and began to move in a slow line along their trail toward the shed.

Sometimes when I came from El Paso for a visit I would help my father with the odds and ends of maintenance around the cabin. About a month before he had his stroke we put shingles on the roof of the hay shed. It was a blazing summer afternoon, and his faded khaki shirt, unbuttoned down his chest, was dark with sweat. We banged away at the shingles, paused now and then to rest and look out over the pastures, and used that vacant time to touch on hard-to-discuss family matters. He always seemed to talk more freely with a hammer in his hand, and it was as if the roof was a proper location for him to deal with things father-to-son.

The hay bales at the shed finally tumbled down and probably became home territory for the field mice. I seldom went out to the barn anymore. I would rather sit beside the cabin, in the shade of the shin oak, and stay focused on the present, the living: the cows cropping grass and slowly licking their calves, the black squirrels bouncing along the fenceline and then scooting up the branches of the walnut trees to spend the afternoon.

Of a Mouse and Me

On a mid-July morning I was reading on the front porch slab of the cabin when a mouse came out from a crack in the wall. He was a wee beastie, as Robert Burns would have said—about half the size of my thumb—and his long trailing tail looked like the queue of hair that young men had begun to wear at the back of the neck.

At first I thought he was just looking for adventure: a mild, baby-mouse kind of exploration along the side of the shaded tin wall. But after watching him a while I understood his mission. He had eaten my Decon-poisoned grain and was on his death march.

Field mice had been invading the cabin at night, and I had finally decided that enough was enough. I put Decon paper trays under a table and waited. The mice had been making themselves very comfortable in my sack of groceries—and one had even become a fan of chocolate chip cookies. (I would lie on my sleeping bag in the dark and listen to him rattling around in the sack, gorging himself. When I shone my flashlight across the cabin he appeared for a moment at the top of the sack—hanging there with a kind of bemused, tolerant expression—then went back down to his midnight feast.)

I put my book aside and bent down to look closer at my porch visitor. The little guy would move and stop, move and stop, not knowing what was giving him such a stomach-ache. ("Is this the normal way to grow up and be a field mouse, Ma, or what?") Not mouselike yet in climbing or cavorting, he was just a hump and tail, a kind of tadpole mouse edging himself along the cabin wall.

When I got down on my knees I could see that his eyes were closed. Either he had shut them against the death agony or he had not yet opened them after birth, had never seen the world he was going to die in. He had begun to tremble and twitch, like a little old man with bad dreams nodding in a chair. As the sow bugs—gray, relentless eighteen-wheelers on their personal interstate across the concrete floor—passed over his tail, the mouse would flinch blindly, then face another direction and sink back into his private quivers. Every now and then when he got an itch he scratched himself with his perfectly shaped field mouse feet—lightning fast, it seemed to me, for so comatose a creature.

After a while I got up and went about my business— cutting weeds around the cabin, drinking coffee, straightening up a wire fence. I checked on Mouse once to see how he was doing, but he was gone—had bumped his way back into a hole in the wall, I assumed, and was somewhere beneath the cabin.

At noon I went to the windmill in the cabin lot, got a long drink of well water, looked at the fat red cows resting under the oaks. When I came back the mouse was lying on his side in the sun. A still little body on the hot porch slab, he had been made dead by me. I had sowed my seeds and reaped this small harvest. He had taken the poison-dusted grain that his mother—good provider that she was—had brought to her children, and—good son that he was—he had dutifully eaten it.

Stretched out on his side, he looked larger, more mouse-like in shape. He had an impressive kind of mouse dignity: front feet formally together, touching one another; ears flattened; fur neat; tail curved down in a proper symmetry. And of course the eyes were still closed. Mouse's brief span of days had been completed in darkness, and he was unaware that he cast no shadow in the blazing summer sun.

When is a death important, I wondered. If an elephant had just died in the cabin yard, would that have been a more notable occurrence? Do we mourn according to size? Albert Schweitzer thought all life to be sacred, but would even he have drawn the line at this hunting cabin mouse?

I looked at the gray form on the slab and thought about life and death of all sizes and in all places, trying to imagine how significant a shadow my own corpse would cast someday beneath the unrelenting sun of our outward-rushing galaxy.

The Sun

The sun—our source, our everything—was out there on the horizon, huge and dusty and bloody red that July afternoon, but no one traveling I-10 seemed to be paying it any mind. Cars were not swerving to the side of the interstate, lining it by the hundreds, the thousands. People were not paused, bumper to bumper: awestruck, sunstruck. They were not squinting in wonder toward the west, marveling and "sore afraid."

It was not, of course, Stonehenge or Babylon or Jericho. It was Leon Springs just north of San Antonio, and all the people in the rush-hour traffic were hurtling along toward their end-of-the-day rendezvous.

The sun: yes, it loomed immense in the horizon's strangely darkened haze and, yes, its outline was as geometrically precise as an interplanetary basketball. But, after all, the travelers on I-10 were not pilgrims or aborigines or Druid priests, and the sun they glanced at was merely that—the sun, familiar and forgettable. It was exploding and burning some 93,000,000 miles away, looking like the red giant it would become someday when it burned the earth's oceans into clouds of steam and caused molten lead to ooze out of the earth's core. But so what? To modern Americans in Broncos and Trans Ams it was hardly worth a second glance. At the end of a summer day it was no more interesting than gravity.

Memories and Moments

Sometimes as a boy I would stand on the Gilmer Street front porch in my leather jacket and smell the smoke from burning leaves and hear the dogs barking in the neighborhood. They were not just smells and sounds, not just isolated features of a fall morning. To me they were fall, the essence of it.

Fall meant an excitement in the air. The leaves of the oak trees in the front yard seemed to be saying something in their shaking. I half-expected the trees themselves to stretch, wave their limbs about, and yawn.

I think it was the recall of earlier, less than tranquil times when I was growing up—when the house was filled with slamming doors, my mother crying in the bedroom, the subsequent great silences—that made us later adopt poses of controlled carefulness with each other. We picked selectively—my mother, brother, and I (my father was on another wavelength)—from a narrowed list of possible emotional responses. We avoided enthusiasms with each other; in place of family openness we substituted a kind of mock world-weariness that passed for candor. (My mother: I had no clear picture of her in my mind despite the various photographs in the family albums. She loomed in my memory as a force, an embodiment of attitudes and emotional states. She was my mother for so many formative years that I could never write sensibly, accurately about who she was as a person, as an individual distinct from her mother-ness. I could not separate her from me.)

As I drove to Bandera early one morning I watched the land slowly reveal itself out of the darkness. The November sky was overcast; the sun had not come up. A lightbulb still burned above the door of a barn near the road, but the coming daylight made the light seem alien, out of place.

Suddenly a bloody splash of the sun emerged through the roadside cedars and oaks: a jolting reminder that the Bandera highway, the hill country, the earth — my life as I drove along — depended on that quarter-sized circle of red now probing its way through the trees.

Trees — just ordinary roadside and pasture trees — were like trees of light in the summer sun. As I went along hill country roads and looked at them, and at pastureland, it was as if I had just been born, had suddenly been given eyes. What more could a human want than to be in the hill country and look out a car window in July at fields, at grass? Every inch of the day astonished me.

I drove and I had, I knew, an enormous secret: I was, once again, a private witness to the blazing radiance of the earth.

In December the Guadalupe River went into a deep coma and lay deserted, except for a few riverbank sparrows who, were they less frivolous, might be tempted to hold some sort of wake for their good departed friend. But they darted about in play, ignoring the bleak banks, swooping in and out of the ragged limbs of the cypress trees (those stately, abandoned members of the Guadalupe's summertime aristocracy).

Sometimes they flocked to a few hollow reeds and tried to enlist them in their games, but they soon understood that the reeds were a weak and lackluster bunch, offering no fun, and they burst into the overcast sky, leaving the reeds to wobble in recoil like abandoned lovers.

I stood outside the hunting cabin drinking coffee and listening to the afternoon. At four o'clock the sky was overcast and there were no bird sounds, no sense of creatures moving about privately in the woods. There was no breeze for the windmill; the trees were bare of leaves. I stood holding the coffee cup, absorbing the silence.

The coals of the small campfire made brief cooling and crackling sounds. Behind the cabin a single brown bird fussed a moment in the woodpile. An owl hooted from a hill.

Then the silence returned.

When it was nearly dark the goats began to trail in toward the cabin lot from the east pasture. I heard a brief snort, then a bell—faintly, like ice being shaken in a metal glass.

The owl hooted once more. Night crickets began. The silence pulsed in the air, joining me to the cold and the land and the descending dark.

Outsider

Paused on Houston Street in San Antonio, I decided to go inside the Gunter Hotel. I stood for a while in the lobby— and looked with a kind of double vision. I was watching and feeling with the same eyes and emotions I had as a child. I was the same funnel through which long-past events and sensations had flowed.

I was still that boy waiting for my Uncle Mitch. I was still all eyes and ears. I saw the light shining on the soft leather sofas and chairs and the bellhops standing in the arched stone doorways in their red-and-blue uniforms. I saw the clusters of businessmen in suits, cigars in their mouths, hands on one another's shoulders. I heard the dim whir of motors and fans deep within the building, the honking of noonday horns out on Houston Street. I smelled lint from the expensive carpet and food from thecoffee shop. I looked at the pictures in their heavy frames along the wall and the huge flags jutting from the mezzanine.

And it had no more significance for me than it did when I was a boy. It was simply the way a hotel lobby was—fascinating, as life was, but without any clear meaning. There was still no fundamental connection between me and the lobby, between me and life. I watched—and was no longer waiting for an uncle, or even for a Godot. I was simply me: intrigued, an outsider.

The House in Fredericksburg

After my divorce, when I was transient and uprooted, the idea of anyone continuing to live in the old traditional way—day after day, year after year in the same house in the same neighborhood—seemed amazing.

One summer day I drove from San Antonio to Fredericksburg and started walking aimlessly along the tree-lined side streets. At a white corner house sitting in the shade of tall pecan trees I stopped and stared. Imagine living there in that same house for the past thirty, forty, fifty years, I thought, experiencing every day the same slanting afternoon sunlight as it came through the same branches of the pecan limbs at a quarter to five. Imagine coming out of the front door and standing for a moment on that same front porch next to the rosebushes in the same familiar flower bed, then going out along the same flagstone walk to the mailbox at the front of the yard and returning to the house and sitting down in the same living room chair and reading letters by the same light coming in at the same angle of the Venetian blinds.

And here I am, I thought, in my midfifties, having more or less wrapped my life in a bandanna and slung it across my shoulder with a piece of frayed rope. I have become, once again, a walker of random roads, an inhabitant of no place and anywhere, possessing only the special wealth of personal freedom. Yet over there, in that white corner house, is someone who, for the past decades, has been a part of an unvarying landscape: belonging intimately, like a farmer in his fields, to his chosen plot of ground.

I walked on, a middle-aged rolling stone.

New Year's Day

In the early morning at the hunting cabin there had been ice on the water troughs, but by noon the wind had died down and the sun came out. I built a fire in the cabin woodstove and watched the pine blocks pop in the flames. Then I went outside and drank coffee in the winter stillness.

The pale midday sun held us — the land, its creatures — suspended in a quiet light. The Hereford cows in the water lot seemed not to breathe; they were as still as cows in a painting. A calf stood with its nose touching a tree, as if receiving a blessing from its friend, the bark. Rounded white rocks in the bed of a nearby arroyo shone like polished bones left by some long-forgotten race.

For a while nothing moved. We were like winter seeds, germinating among the subdued browns of the pasture.

When the spell of the moment was broken, I went back into the cabin, smiling. I smiled because of the way the sharp winter air had felt on my face; because of how the cows looked — all soberly passive, all facing in the same direction, as if waiting for the arrival of some inspirational leader who was going to bring them the annual Cow Address; because of the good smell of the wood smoke, and the good feel of my old K-Mart jacket; because of the way the sun, millions of miles away, came through the doorway like a personal friend in order to spread an intimate shine on the bare cedar desk.

A cabin in the hill country surrounded by trees—it was the right place to be on New Year's Day. It was as I had known for a long while: the countryside could always provide me the sense of a new beginning, today or any day of the year.

Grief

Ernestine Bierschwale Wagner Hurst, in her seventies, lost her third husband during the summer. Leukemia. Not many people recognized the Hurst name when they read about it in the newspaper, Ernestine told me. They knew her as Bierschwale or Wagner.

We were in the Stop-and-Shop barbecue place outside Kerrville one August afternoon. I was on my way to the hunting cabin and was waiting for half a pound of sliced beef when she came in to order sausage. She had always been a smiler—that was her trademark—and the tendency to smile was still there as we talked. She had lost her husband, but no one who had read the newspaper knew it was *her* husband. Not many knew she had married again after Lester Wagner died. She wanted to tell me about it there by the doughnut tray while we waited.

"I guess you know I lost my husband."

"No," I said. "I'm sorry. I've just been in town on a little visit."

"Yes, it was three months ago."

The clerk handed me my sliced beef and I held it, hot in its sack, while we talked. Ernestine Bierschwale—as I had known her for most of my life—was related to my family by marriage and she had always been there at the big reunions I'd gone to with my family years ago. I had moved away from the hill country after college, but whenever I was back in town during the summer or at Christmas I would sometimes cash a check at the bank downtown where she worked. I would go to her window and we would talk about kinfolks and the weather after she counted out my money. She always smiled her big, loose-lipped, pleasant smile. Her teller's nameplate changed over the years from Bierschwale to Wagner, but she retired before needing to change it again.

She had survived three husbands and did not quite know what to do about it. That's how it seemed to me. She wanted people to know what had happened to her: in just a year and a half, the third husband was gone too, and now after all those years of husbands she was without one and probably would not have another one again. She was finally going to be alone, and she wanted people to know about it—the news, the loss.

I held my sack of sliced barbecue until I finally didn't know what else to say. We didn't have more than just a passing friendship—just the periodic formality of inquiring about each other's family. And she did not seem inconsolably grief-stricken. She just seemed dazed and a bit lost.

When I left, Ernestine's fixed, bank teller's smile was back in place as she waited for the counter girl to finish wrapping her two links of sausage.

"Tell Me Something"

I lived alone, and every morning in San Antonio I got up and drove to school from an empty apartment. I worked steadily, doggedly, at the job of being a teacher. Then, at five o'clock, my school day over, I walked out toward my car—and a sense of emotional devastation. With each step my teacher's iron mantle slipped from me, so that by the time I had reached the car I was no longer a public person; I was once again privately me. My body was like a huge mouth, tasting gall.

I put the key into the door of the car, and I thought about the long hours that remained before bedtime, and I said it: "I hate my life. I hate the way I live." And as I drove slowly across the parking lot I did not have a sense of commitment, of connection, of interest or goal, of belonging to anybody or any place.

One afternoon I drove up into the countryside of Bulverde and parked beside a field. I sat in my car with the window rolled down. I was alone, desperate. Nothing—not reading, thinking, patiently waiting—worked for me anymore. I was a stripped nub, with no green vines growing.

I looked at the familiar pastureland in the late afternoon light, and I began to speak to the trees, the rocks, the air. I had nowhere else to turn.

It was not like trying to talk to God. Long ago I had stopped calling out to a Force in the world. It was more like an Indian might call out to his brother, the bear. I wanted, I suppose, some sign of kinship from the Created rather than from a Creator — a recognition of our common fate.

"Tell me something," I said, meaning, "I'm lost, I can't go on."

The small cedar saplings kept up their enigmatic nodding in the breeze. That was all the answer I got.

Just before dark I drove to the little crossroads convenience store in Bulverde and parked out front under an oak tree. I watched through the store window: a gray-haired man in his seventies drank from a can of Coors as he sat in a curved-back chair. He was talking to the cashier, a young woman in a red-and-brown checked shirt. Every now and then they laughed at what the man was saying.

As customers stopped to buy gas, newspapers, snuff, fried pies, six packs, the gray-haired man continued to sit in his chair, smiling, sometimes leaning back into the rack of potato chips and gazing about the store, sometimes facing forward, talking again to the cashier. Every once in a while, between customers, the young woman cut off slices from a round of cheese on the counter, handed a piece to the man, kept one for herself, leaned forward across the counter on her elbows.

More than anything else I wanted to go inside, pull up another chair, and have a can of Coors with the cashier and the gray-haired man, just be there inside where the bright store lights burned and listen to their idle talk as the shadows filled the trees outside and the overcast October afternoon turned to night.

Home Town Revisited

I drove up to Kerrville and walked among the browns of winter along streets of my home town. December trees — stark, leafless, awkward, bare — reached up, reached out, but they had nothing to offer the cold midday sky. Brown leaves lay like crinkled memories scattered and forgotten along the curb.

In my old neighborhood I stood at the intersection of Gilmer Street and Third, and it was like a wound that had never healed. There, behind the rotting picket fence, under the huge live oaks, was the home place. (I was a child forever beneath those trees, and that child is buried in me still.) I stared ahead, trying to decipher all the hidden messages written in wintertime sun-and-shadow.

A man drove by in a red Toyota, and it was my father — fifty years ago — that I saw at the wheel. It was the wrong car going too fast, but it was the right zipper jacket he was wearing and the right gray felt hat. It was the same profile, the same eyebrows, the same darting, restless eyes.

Three blocks away were the fields — still vacant at the edge of town — where we went each Christmas, my father and I, to cut a cedar tree for our living room. We went after work, after he had closed his feed store, and we drove across Quinlan Creek and parked the truck, and we climbed through the wire fence just at dark and picked out a small, properly shaped tree and chopped it down. As we put the tree in the back of the truck, I smelled the cedar resin in the cold December air. I saw the lights coming on across town. Dogs barked. I could hear fireworks in the neighborhood. My father had lit his cigar and I smelled it in the cold air. I did not know, of course, that this was one of a thousand such moments I would remember when I was grown: the two of us in the cab, bouncing along in the old pickup, the dim headlights leading us home along the rocky, unpaved street.

Yes, I was there again in my home town, but I was not.

I lived there once; I never did.

I left; I never quite went away.

My parents are dead and gone; their lives live on.

Plenty of Juice and Rest

My week at the cabin had started off routinely. I wrote a bit on a story, cleaned the outhouse, chopped away a few cedars from the rim of the cow pond in the east pasture, took a walk down the walnut-bordered arroyo below the cabin.

At noon I went up to Harper, bought a watermelon, idled through Mr. Grona's lumberyard and ended up buying a sack of fence staples. I bought a hamburger and a fried pie at the Longhorn Inn Cafe and then spent the afternoon wandering down paved and unpaved country roads.

Just before dark I drove back to the cabin. Bright-green sumacs lined the road. Angora goats were stretching through pasture fences to the luring grasses on the other side.

I read outside the cabin doorway for a while by the light of the Coleman lantern, then turned it off and sat in darkness. I looked up at the hill country section of the universe above me and tried, once again, to think about it: the stars, the universe, my life, any life. Once again I did not get very far with that kind of thinking, so I took the lantern inside and went to bed.

At midnight I woke with violent chills and fever. I shivered and thrashed around on the bunk bed. My head throbbed. I covered myself with a sleeping bag but jerked and quivered as the chills continued.

The next day I sat around the cabin nursing my misery. Summer flu, I told myself—some kind of virus. Just have to wait it out. I drank fruit juice and took aspirin and lay on the bed. My head and body ached. My stomach hurt.

The following day, Wednesday, I drove into Kerrville. In the doctor's waiting room I tried to scan the pages of a magazine, but I gave up and sat there, feverish, staring dully ahead. The doctor examined me, agreed with my self-diagnosis of summer flu, recommended that I keep up the juices and get lots of rest.

On the way out of town I telephoned Deborah, my daughter, who lived in San Antonio, and told her I was feeling pretty punk and probably wouldn't be seeing her until the following week. I bought more cans of fruit juice and went back to the cabin.

Thursday and Friday I drank the juices, lay on my bed, and ached. Friday afternoon I managed to put myself in the car and let it drive itself to a crossroads pay phone. I called my daughter. She said, "Why don't you just come on down to my apartment? It will be cooler and more comfortable." I told her I felt too lousy to drive. But I would be all right, I assured her; the flu just takes time. I made it back to the cabin. I ached; my head throbbed. My stomach still hurt.

Saturday was a summer scorcher, and I lay like an empty sack on the cabin bed and sweated. My headache was worse. In midafternoon I heard a series of cheery honks as a car wound down the rocky pasture road toward the cabin.

"I just had a hunch I ought to come up and get you, Pops," my daughter said in the doorway. I looked up from my bunk and didn't argue. I stuffed a few clothes into a sack, closed up the cabin, and walked my sick man's walk out to Deborah's car.

In Kerrville we stopped by the hospital. I called my doctor's number, but there was no answer. A doctor in the emergency room examined me. Yes-sir, he said, probably a virus. Get lots of rest and be sure to take plenty of liquids.

I dressed behind the curtain of the cubicle. My daughter and I went on to San Antonio.

Deborah's apartment was pleasant and cool, but it didn't make me feel any better. I took Tylenol, but it didn't touch the headache. Or the chills. Late that afternoon I was sitting on the couch in a kind of stoic stupefaction when I began to shake. I got up, thinking, I guess, that I could somehow control the shaking better if I were on my feet. But I was like a paint can that had been placed on an electric vibrator in order to mix the paint. I thought I was going to shake apart.

Sunday morning Deborah drove me to a nearby drop-in clinic. The pleasant young doctor on duty—very young; I might have been the second or third patient of his brief career—examined me and ran a few tests. Deborah and I waited for the results. He came back to the small, white-walled room and told us that I had nothing to worry about. I, indeed, had a troublesome case of flu. I should take plenty of liquids and get lots of rest. After I wrote him a check Deborah drove me back to her apartment.

I don't remember many details of that Sunday night. I know my head had become a balloon that would soon burst, and I had recurrent episodes of the paint-can shakes.

About five o'clock Monday morning I woke Deborah and said, "Let's go." She drove me to the emergency room of Northeast Baptist Hospital where a chart was begun for "an extremely ill fifty-six-year-old gentleman."

Meningitis? Maybe. The medical staff couldn't be certain at first, but they had guesses—educated guesses. The doctor on duty was struck by the similarity of my symptoms to those of patients he had been reading about just the night before in the *New England Journal of Medicine*. The preliminary work was begun immediately: spinal tap, X-rays, blood tests, sonar investigations of the stomach. At some point during the day the early morning diagnosis proved correct: I had Rocky Mountain spotted fever. Caused by ticks. Ticks at the cabin.

The following ten days in and out of intensive care were a blur of white-coated doctors standing by my bedside during the day and nurses holding little cups of pills during the surrealistic nights; of CAT scans and catheters and IVs and bedpans and drip morphine for the raging headache that would not ease. My internal organs were in a state of sepsis, I was told later—swollen, haywire, messed up by the poisons of the infection.

Finally the antibiotics did their work. My headache subsided to a tolerable throb, I glanced at the front page of a newspaper, I was able to sit up and accept my reward of hospital food that smelled and tasted like Styrofoam that had been liberally seasoned with Styrofoam herbs and then cooked in a deep Styrofoam oven.

When it was smiles-and-check-out time, the doctor in charge looked at me and said, "It will be a couple of months before you feel like yourself again. You know, if you had waited another twenty-four hours we probably couldn't have saved you."

I nodded, thanked him, and thought of the cans of fruit juice still lined up at the cabin.

Fall Afternoon

It was late on a Friday afternoon in October. I had finished another week of teaching and was headed north out of San Antonio. The highway was smooth beneath my wheels, and the cooling air came through the open windows. The sun was low but still bright on the fields. At turns in the road the sun rays slanted and glittered through the bordering trees, across barns and windmills.

Friday afternoon — the end of another work week — and as I drove along it was as if I were gliding through every fall afternoon I had ever known, as if the essences of fall were concentrated among the shadows edging into the roadside. I watched the yellow school buses turn off the farm-to-market road onto country lanes. I passed little crossroad stores. I drove slowly through the October shadow-and-light, and I could smell the creek bottoms when I dipped down and crossed low-water bridges. Lightning bugs were beginning to blink in the distance, and the oak trees and their shadows kept marking my passage like patient, serene sentinels.

Near Fredericksburg I pulled off the road and stared at a farmhouse. Newly painted and trimmed, it sat back from the road behind a row of large, evenly spaced pecan trees. The tin-roofed front porch rested on four white wooden columns. A Border collie lay beside the steps near the flower bed, watching as a ewe and her lamb grazed in the front yard grass.

It was as if I had paused in front of a modest hill country utopia. The grazing sheep, the shade-spreading pecan trees, the backyard garden and windmill, the low nearby hills—they seemed to be offering tired travelers a way station at the end of the day. I half-expected the front door to open and a portly, smiling German farmer, pipe in one hand, the other raised in greeting, to stand there, waiting for me to join him in a glass of beer and maybe a game of croquet on the lawn before dark.

Meditation on a Photograph

I was seated at my desk when I glanced up from the typewriter to a framed picture on the wall. It was a composite of three photographs spliced together so that it stretched out like one of those wide-angle pictures made of a high school graduating class. The picture showed a dozen or so Hereford cows, grazing during a summer afternoon in front of the hunting cabin.

I looked at the sleek-bellied Herefords, the live oaks and their pools of shade, the background greenery of the other pasture live oaks, cedars, and sycamores. It was a ranchland pastoral that had been a part of my life since childhood. As I stared at it—framed, familiar, serene—I tried to plumb its depths.

I got up, stood closer. On the summer day when the photograph was taken, I was just out of camera range, and now I was inches away from those same imperturbable cows that—noses to the grass—were still oblivious of the rusted barrel beside the fence, the logs of the back-lot corral, the arching live oak limbs, the sunlight and the afternoon shadows.

What was going on that day? What remained unspoken about it that still needed to be said?

I had sat in the cabin doorway on a similar summer day, reading the letters of Isak Dinesen to her friends and family. She wrote about the animals, the people, the landscapes of her farm in Kenya as she later wrote about them in *Out of Africa*. I had closed the book, thinking that without too much of a shift her descriptions would have been appropriate for the very hills and pastures and arroyos that stretched around me.

I turned from the picture to other things. Days passed. Then, reading a letter Henry Miller once wrote to Anaïs Nin, I came to understand that the picture was my own unrecoverable Eden. Miller had written that in the beginning, yes, there was the Word, but for the Word to appear there had to be a parting, a separation from the original innocence, and that the Word is always seeking out the first, more perfect condition.

In my cabin-lot picture the red cows, the constant trees, and the summer sky are as silent as Adam: beyond the reach of words. They are in their timeless equilibrium, separate and perfect, forever lost to me behind glass.

Partners

It is perhaps just a matter of my seeing something and superimposing my emotions on what I see. Perhaps it is simply this: my responding intensely to what is, to me, the mood of a thing that, to another, has no mood, no mysterious hidden depth, and is just the ordinary moodless object that everyone else sees and gives only a passing glance.

I am talking here about a house I saw one late summer afternoon, sitting by itself along a country road. I had stopped my car and was looking at the neat house and yard there in the long stretch of fields, and it was as if the house was as much afternoon as it was house, as if the afternoon had imprinted itself on the front wall and windows and door, the adjoining garage, the side slab of smooth cement now in shadow, the line of small trees and grass.

I'm saying that even though it was six o'clock or so, with the sun setting low over the fields, the afternoon still seemed to be an almost tangible presence. It was as if the three and four and five o'clock hours had not disappeared but through some kind of subtle chemistry had transformed themselves into boards and bricks and cement and had assumed the shape of that silent house and yard. It was as if the house and the afternoon were patient partners who—quietly alone with each other during the long, vacant hours along that hot country road—shared what the other had to offer. The house offered its form, its physical shape, to the formless, eternal afternoon, and together, as one—as intimate companions—they waited there beneath the pecan trees for the gradually approaching night.

In Center Point

Alone and despondent, I wondered how it would be to go live in Center Point, near Kerrville, and find a house on a small lot with a modest yard, no fence around it, with several pecan trees near the street.

I could go there and turn my back on all that I once had been, on what I had tried to be in my life. I would try to shrink my awareness and live simply in this pecan-shaded, unprepossessing place.

I would be there in the spring, near the river, standing under my trees on my narrow street.

I would look out the kitchen window and see the tomatoes growing in the back garden.

I would be private, limited, circumscribed.

But first I would get into the car and drive down side roads past the maize fields of Center Point in the spring sun. I would see the sunflowers along the fences and cedar trees on the nearby hills.

I would turn onto the lane I remembered from years before that ran straight for a while between the fields and then gradually climbed through roadside oaks and sycamores. As it wound along, leaving the fields, entering the privateness of the low caliche hills, I would look out at the shaded places among the cedars and then I would stop the car.

I would get out and stand in the intimate, familiar stillness of the afternoon. I would be again in a personal place that—like so many other countryside, personal places I had sought out over the years—seemed to have buried within it the truths I was searching for. I would stand a final time near the sun-warmed trees and grasses and let the silence of the moment tell me that no answers had been waiting for me there, or anywhere.

I would drive back to my frame house in Center Point and sit for a while on the front porch as the afternoon faded into hill country darkness. I would listen to the night birds begin, then get up, go inside, close the door, and try not to think anymore.

Remembering Carlton Stokes

I sat and I thought about the hill country—my growing-up days, my family and relatives, all the country people and the country places—and I did not think I could function if I stayed there any longer. Memories weighed too much.

I started to think about Carlton Stokes and the shape of his life. I picked up a pen and started to write.

As he drove toward his ranch in the June heat, he looked out at the land and it was almost an extension of his body: solid, stable, enduring. The pastures, the fences, the gates—all were as they should be; all were as familiar to him as his hands on the steering wheel. Occasionally he glanced out at the cattle in the fields, at the coloring-book blue of the sky. The sun was shining on the oak trees, and their leaves were like mirrors of light.

On this stretch of highway the road from Kerrville to Harper was straight as a ruler, narrowing to a point on the ridge in the distance. From time to time the road eased down into dry branch crossings where the sumacs grew close to the pavement and towering Spanish oaks bent together in shading arches. Carlton Stokes drove into the brief shadows; then his Plymouth rose again into the sunlight of late afternoon. He drove steadily, without hurry. He was comfortable behind the wheel. His Stetson was set squarely above his eyes; his polished boot was pressed firmly against the gas pedal.

He did not feel the fifty-one years of his life. They had

folded naturally, properly into his body, leaving no bothersome trace. He ate well, slept well, bedded well his wife. His livestock had good grass and good water. His fencelines were still stretched tight. And without being told, he knew that he was still a fine figure of a man.

Thinking of the sliced garden tomatoes, roasting ears, and pork chops that he would be having for supper—and then about sitting out on the cool porch slab after sundown in his bare feet, watching the deer graze in the oat field down by the creek—Carlton Stokes pressed a little harder on the pedal.

He lay in the bedroom—the blinds shut against the summer sun—and gasped for breath. The large white mound of his stomach rose and fell, rose and fell, rapidly, through his unbuttoned pajama top. He turned to look at the clock on the bedside table: two-thirty. It was still thirty minutes until he could put on the mask and take his medicated mist treatment. As he leaned back into the pillows the plastic tube from the oxygen tank pinched sharply into his nostrils.

At age eighty-four this was what he was doing now: lying on the bed waiting for the next partial breath, the next partial medical relief. But no breath was ever enough, no relief lasted. His emphysema and his asthma clamped his chest and would not let go. He reared back with each half-breath, his face and nose distorted into puffy caricatures, his once-handsome features swollen by prednisone. He could still make it to the bathroom by himself and could still lie for a while on the couch in the front room to watch a little television. But there wasn't much left in his life that he could do, or cared to do.

He heard his neighbor's pickup drive up the hill and park out front. Carlton called his wife's name: not a yell, just a strained burble of a cough. He waited, then called again. He heard the door of the pickup slam and then Milton Weatherby's boots coming up the front walk. As Carlton was calling again, his wife was already wheeling herself slowly out of the guest bedroom that was now her own. She inched forward past the dining table and the TV set toward the front door.

Milton Weatherby knocked, waited, then knocked again as he began to open the door. He was carrying a paper sack of peaches he had picked that morning from his trees. He came inside and put the peaches on the table, saying hello to Carlton's wife as she held out her hand to him from the wheelchair. Milton Weatherby had started talking about the noon weather report when both of them heard the sound and turned, looking toward Carlton Stokes.

He had gotten himself out of bed—to visit a bit, to be social—but this afternoon the getting up was more than he could handle. He held on to the bedroom doorway, trailing his oxygen tube. He was heaving and gasping, throwing his head back, his white hair wild, his stomach bulging out of his pajamas.

Milton Weatherby rushed toward him as Carlton's wife, her hands together in her lap, began saying over and over, in a level, almost monotonous voice, as if speaking to a terrified child, "It will be all right, Carlton." As if she really believed it would be, or as if the time had long ago passed when what she said made any difference.

Home Again

In the dead-brown of winter I came back from central Texas to the Lower Valley of the Rio Grande—to desert sand, to flatness and fields, to mountains in the distance. After long hours of driving I stopped my car—near Fort Hancock, at a dry canal by the side of the road—and in the late afternoon stood beneath a cottonwood. With the land quietening, with no breeze stirring, the words rose up within me like a testimonial, and I thought them in the cooling afternoon: "I'm home."

I had left all of it—the loneliness and despondency, the brooding and fumbling about—and had come back west where I belonged.

I had not thought it possible to do that. I had for too long accepted the credo of Thomas Wolfe, "You can't go home again," as a truth for me—but it wasn't. El Paso was where I belonged—where any day could seem like the fresh, first day of the world, not a worn carbon copy.

I drove on to Clint to be in touch again with its small-town pleasures. I walked along the canal, and the clumps of yellowed grass in the sandy ground, the half-buried beer tabs, the broken plastic spoons were somehow reassuring—like the household objects of old friends. I looked out at the fields as they lay, at dusk, in a kind of pale, cinnamon sunlight, intersected here and there by tree shadows from the canal.

At a convenience store along the highway that runs through town I sat in my car, sipping a bourbon-and-Coke from a plastic cup. I tipped the cup toward a dumpster in a bit of a homecoming toast. Boys in baseball caps walked into the store, came out later with sodas in big plastic bottles. They went back across the nearby ditch—disappeared into it for a moment, just their caps visible—and returned home. I watched them, Clint guys on a winter afternoon, and tried to imagine them, their lives, as they grew up there in a small, bypassed, cotton-growing valley town.

After dark I headed toward El Paso. On the left was Mexico and the long, unbroken border horizon: the desert land at early nighttime lit, as if in an unending Christmas celebration, by the feast of Juárez and El Paso lights. I could see Mount Franklin in the distance, a sphinxlike reminder of things that last: a fixed place in the universe, the mountain that meant home.

Looking for Byron

On January 26, 1999, my son, Byron, thirty years old, drove away from his mother's house in east San Antonio in his green pickup truck, headed for a halfway house downtown. But he did not go there. He disappeared. Over six months passed, and no one in his family saw him after that January afternoon.

Until his midtwenties Byron was simply Byron, the engaging, pleasant-featured son that I loved. His mother, Judy, and I had divorced when he was eleven, and yes, that had been painful and disturbing to him. But he seemed to handle the situation well enough. He graduated from high school, went on to college — even considered entering medical school and perhaps becoming an emergency room physician. Then one night in San Marcos eight years ago a hit-and-run driver ran into him while he was walking with friends. He suffered a closed-head injury that caused him to lose certain memory functions as well as his sense of smell. To add a classic insult to injury, he was shortly thereafter diagnosed as having a manic-depressive disorder.

Suddenly the whole trajectory of his life changed. He was unable to function alone, so he moved from his San Marcos apartment to his mother's house in San Antonio. He suffered dizzy spells; he had double-vision problems. He went regularly to psychiatrists and psychotherapists for treatment and was placed on a number of medications to treat his obsessive-compulsive behavior and depression:

Tegretol, Depakote, Klonopin, lithium. He became a recluse in his room, staying in bed for long stretches of time, his mother's Boston terrier asleep beside him. He lost interest in his song writing and guitar playing—for which he had an undeniable talent.

To self-medicate his despair, he began to take cocaine. Lots of it. He became an addict.

In June 1998 Judy and I entered him into a private rehabilitation hospital in San Antonio. He stayed there for a month, and when he left he seemed positive again about his future—even though we were told by his therapist that the relapse rate for cocaine addicts is almost 90 percent.

He worked around the yard at Judy's house, enjoyed the dogs and his music. But by the end of the year old patterns reasserted themselves: he started forging checks and stealing money from Judy in order to buy cocaine.

By mid-January Judy felt she was at her wit's end, exhausted and depressed herself from dealing with Byron. With the help of his therapist she located a halfway house near Cypress Street and San Pedro Avenue. He was to go there and try to put some pieces of his life together.

But he didn't really want to go. Visibly depressed, Judy said later, he put canned goods from the kitchen into a plastic container, carried the basket to his truck—which needed repairs and no longer worked in reverse—and with fourteen dollars in his wallet took off down the street.

He never showed up at the halfway house.

Judy called me in El Paso. We talked. We tried to make sense out of what had happened: where he had gone, how he would live, what he would do when he ran out of his medication, which he carried with him in a strap-on pouch. She felt he might be suicidal.

We waited, hoping that in a few days he would call. He didn't. Should we make contact with the police and list him as missing? Where was he spending the nights, which had turned cold?

I called Joe Esquell, a hill country rancher who now leased the hunting cabin property from me near Kerrville. I told him that Byron had disappeared and might drive up from San Antonio to our cabin place and, well, I explained, he was very depressed. Would Joe please drive down and check to see if Byron was there, and then call me?

Mr. Esquell telephoned me that night. He said he and his wife had driven around in the pastures before dark but did not see any sign of Byron's truck.

We listed Byron as a missing person with the San Antonio police department. He was put on N.C.I.C., the nationwide computer database. We contacted his friends. No one had seen him.

I went to San Antonio, and Judy and I made a missing person's flyer with a sideview photograph of Byron— smooth-shaven, hair pulled back in a ponytail, a pleasing profile. It gave pertinent information and also stated: "$1,000 reward for specific information resulting in his safe return." We distributed the flyers in various neighborhoods.

For hours I drove aimlessly, doggedly—looking into driveways and backyards for a green truck—returning, driving the same streets once more. I would stop where I saw a man pulling weeds at his front sidewalk, get out, show him the flyer with Byron's picture, tell him I was looking for my son, who had a head injury and had disappeared from home and might not have access to his medication. The man would give the flyer a long look, slowly shake his head. No, he hadn't seen him. I would drive some more, stop where a man was playing street football with a few kids, lean out the window and show the flyer. Nope, didn't recognize him.

A woman called, saying she had seen the flyer I had taped in the front area of a Wal-Mart, then had later noticed someone resembling Byron at the Eisenhauer Road flea market. She said she couldn't help noticing the intense stare of his blue eyes. It made a kind of sense: Byron maybe needing to buy some cheap used clothes, or maybe just wanting a place to hang out inconspicuously among crowds of people drifting about, looking for bargains.

I circled the flea market parking lot, looking for his truck, then walked for a couple of hours in the huge market itself and tacked up flyers on bulletin boards. I took a staple gun and spent the afternoon attaching flyers to telephone poles in the area. I left flyers at stop-and-shop convenience stores.

After dark I sat in the car, thinking, Maybe if I just get out and stand on a street corner; maybe if I yell out, as loud as I can, "By-ron!" Maybe that is all that is left to do. Maybe somewhere, wherever he is, he will hear me, and he will know I am out here in the night, looking for him, and it will break the spell of silence that has settled around him.

Each day in March, each day in April: nothing. The San Antonio morgue still had no unidentified bodies.

What to do next? My periodic calls to his friends—Any word about Byron?—were met with the same monotonous replies: No, nothing. Finally they became pointless.

Maybe he had overdosed or mixed his medications, if he still had any, in a fatal combination with cocaine or had been bludgeoned in a drug encounter gone wrong. Did he even have any of his medications? Could he function without them? I called the Eckerd's pharmacy where he had prescriptions filled. No, the pharmacist said, he had not been in for refills.

In May Judy and I decided to go ahead and do it: our last resort was to contact a private investigator. He took the case. June and July passed. We waited. But by August we knew no more about Byron's whereabouts than we had in January.

It was time now, I thought. I had to sell the family ranch

property. I would be needing money to pay for Byron's hospitalization whenever he was found—or perhaps to provide for his long-term rehabilitation. Or I might want to set up a trust fund for him if it turned out he could never be self-supporting. I contacted a broker in Kerrville representing a San Antonio doctor who was interested in buying my land. In late August I signed papers completing the sale.

On the afternoon of September 3 the new owner was taking a walk in the far back part of what had been my property and came across Byron's green truck, with Byron's body—what was left of it—inside. Byron had evidently driven it into a kind of brush cave down below a bluff, making it practically undetectable. He had jammed a black plastic hose into the exhaust pipe, run it into the side of the cab, and committed suicide by inhaling carbon monoxide. The key to the engine was still turned on. He was wrapped in several blankets, apparently against the January or February cold. His strap-on pouch contained his driver's license and prescriptions. The medication bottles scattered about were empty. The basket for groceries was still in the truck.

The autopsy indicated he had been dead for at least six months.

I was not with him. I do not know what he thought about, where he went, how much of his medication—or how much cocaine—he took from his pouch. I don't know where he bought the plastic hose. I don't know when he decided he would make no phone call, would not contact anyone in his family after January 26. I can only imagine them, those final days, his last hours.

His truck was his home now. He lived in it night and day. He drove the San Antonio streets, not yet sure what he was going to do. He drove past familiar places—down San Pedro and past Tiffany's Billiards, past Wal-Mart where he would go late at night to wander the aisles. Around the blocks, down the streets, slowly.

The January nights were getting colder, and in the darkness along Cibolo Creek he lay in the cab, wrapped in his two blankets.

When he knew what he was going to do he got on I-10 and started north. He drove past Boerne and Comfort and Kerrville without slowing down. He turned off I-10 at the farm-to-market road, drove the next two miles, and there was the gate to the ranch property. He unlocked the chain, went along the rocky, caliche road, passing the small valley area where he and I had cooked our camp-out meals years before. He drove on through the cabin lot without stopping—past the windmill and the stock tank, the salt blocks—turned left, followed the dry bed of the arroyo.

He drove deep into the pasture—veering around oaks and sycamores, bouncing over washouts and flint rocks— until he found the spot he was headed for. He swung the truck around, aimed alongside an embankment through tall grass into a heavy stand of cedars.

The truck was hidden now.

He got the plastic hose and inserted it into the exhaust pipe. He stuffed in rags to make it airtight. He ran the hose into the window wing on the driver's side. He pulled off his shoes, wrapped up in his blankets against the cold, turned on the engine, and lay down across the seat of the cab.

I think of the deer that came along the fenceline the next morning, seeing the truck within the cedar cave, standing still as they considered it, moving on. I see the armadillos beginning to rustle in the leaves nearby. A hawk sails overhead. The sun arcs across to the west; doves call from the surrounding oaks at sundown. Nighttime comes, settles over the land, the truck, his body.

I see the repeated cycle of each morning, each day through the spring and summer months, the ranchland accepting, absorbing the secret of his return: Byron, hidden, becoming less and less my son and becoming more and more a corruption of exploding gases and decaying flesh.

He had returned to the countryside to die. He chose what was for him a home place. He drove through familiar gates and down pasture roads, and there he buried himself: his childhood, his dreams, his final, desperate hopelessness. Beneath his two blankets, as alone as anyone can be, he curled himself into the final shape of his life.

Each night I go to bed and I think my stark thoughts of him. Each morning I get up, my thoughts unchanged. I did not know it would be this way: that on one side would be Byron's death and on the other side everything else, that his death would so completely out-balance the rest of life.

Daily routines have lost their resonance. Objects, people, events no longer have shading or shadow. I have stopped listening to music. It seems irrelevant, an extravagance. I prefer the blank emptiness of silence.

Since my early adult life I have looked steadily about me, valuing the sights of the earth. But I no longer can see them, such sights, with my own eyes. I find myself looking into afternoon fields with the eyes of a father whose son did not want to live anymore, and this dead son blocks my vision. I cannot see past him.

Byron's disappearance, the loss of him — the loss of him to *me* — is so profound I cannot process experience anymore. For thirty years I was his father; I assumed I would be his father for the rest of my life. Now I am not, and I have lost the sense of who I am.

I loved him — uninterruptedly, constantly. I took pleasure in the serene knowledge of that love. But death shrivels memory, reduces it so completely that Byron has not only disappeared from the present; he is disappearing from the past. Death is taking his reality away.

He had a need to die. I try to accept the fact that he did not ask me to try to save his life. All I can do now is put these words—like blood—onto paper in an effort to provide for him a kind of wholeness, a justification.